THE SIGN
OF THE SON
OF MAN

GAYLA WISE

Covenant Communications, Inc.

To my brother-in-law, John C. Kinghorn,
a well-read Gospel Doctrine teacher who introduced
me to the term and concept of the Shechinah.
Thanks, John, for the scriptural treasure hunt
that resulted.

Library of Congress Catalog Number 91–072631
The Sign of the Son of Man: "The Shechinah"
Printed September 1991
ISBN 1–55503–358–X

CONTENTS

FOREWORD

This book contains the most complete and clearly written discussion published to date on the glory of the Lord as manifested on the earth. Gayla Wise's work yields another gem of knowledge set in place before the Lord comes in glory to assume the throne of his kingdom. She rightly recognizes that to understand these times we must understand ancient times and duplicate the conditions upon which the Lord acts on behalf of his people. By drawing together all scriptures available on this subject, the author leaves little room for taking an idea out of context. We are on sure ground as she connects evidences of former manifestations of the Lord's presence to those yet to happen. We need only examine the past to see what the future holds; that is a very Jewish way of looking at things.

The narrow kind of result one might expect when a writer focuses on a single idea does not occur here. The idea of the Shechinah—the presence of the Lord in a brilliance of light—ties together many scriptures, such as those that discuss the Lord's covenants, thus allowing us to gain an overall perspective on this subject. The Shechinah fits naturally into the broader context of God's dealings with humanity. If God is going to protect his people with a

pillar of cloud, as Isaiah prophesies (as God protected the Israelites who came out of Egypt), then
who, for example, will qualify for that glorious blessing? By studying the ancient paradigm—by doing a
rhetorical and typological analysis of it in the scriptures—the author tells us in plain terms who will
obtain that protection. Those who keep their
covenants with the Lord will obtain it.

If that idea seems simplistic, scriptural instances
of the divine presence are linked to plenty of flesh-
and-blood examples of those who kept God's commandments and received a visitation from the Lord.
The human paradigms of covenantal righteousness—Enoch, Moses, Elijah, Lehi, Nephi, Joseph
Smith, and others—are as helpful for us to know as
the doctrines they taught and lived that brought
them into the presence of the Lord. If we learn to
live as those who walked and talked with God did,
then surely we will be among those who will wel-
come Jesus when he comes to the earth. Since God is
no respecter of persons, and is the same yesterday,
today, and forever, could we imagine that he would
appear to us if we were not as prepared to see him as
they were? Do we suppose we could endure his presence if we did not measure up to their righteousness?

In Moses' day, the Lord's elect went up on the
Mount with Moses and saw God, while the rest ran
from the mountain for fear of their lives. In the Book
of Mormon, the more righteous part of the Nephites
received the Lord after his resurrection. The rest
were destroyed in the calamities that preceded his
coming. How few people heeded the voice of the
prophets then! And how few understood the divine
revelations and applied them to themselves!

The Shechinah certainly is not an Old Testament
curiosity, an idea we can view superficially and file

in our mental computers. It has to do with the heart of the gospel, with the coming of the Lord to us as individuals and also to us as a people. When the Lord comes (and he *is* coming) he will come as he has in times before. True, this time he will come to more people, to entire nations and kindreds, for the world is a bigger place and the people of God are more numerous. But the manner and conditions of his coming remain the same. We have the scriptures to tell us so.

Gayla Wise has served us well by doing a synopsis of this important subject. As we read the scriptures again after studying the evidence, our minds will be more sensitive to the nuances of meaning that speak of sacred experiences. Spiritual ideas will emerge from the pages that we otherwise might have overlooked. Most of all, by applying the scriptures to ourselves we can begin building a construct of how these things relate to us. What is our goal in the matter? Do we believe such things can and should happen to us? Are we willing to follow the paradigms of those who have made their calling and election sure, who have served the Lord unwearyingly to bring salvation to others? These are the larger questions that should flow out of a study such as this.

This book honors those who enhance the leap of understanding with the leap of faith and works. Upon some of the more imperceptible words and scriptures hinge some of the most profound truths. Their personal revelation to us can impact our lives to ultimately conform with the paradigm of Jesus Christ. When we reach that point, we shall see him as he is.

Avraham Gileadi

1

THE SHECHINAH

When I first heard the word *Shechinah* (*Shə-ˋkē-nə*), my curiosity was piqued. Here was a strange Hebrew word giving a name to the mysterious concept of "a cloud by day and a pillar of fire by night." In English, Shechinah means "the sign of the Son of Man."

When the ancient Israelites escaped Egypt, a strange phenomenon occurred—accompanying them on their journey was a pillar of cloud by day and a pillar of fire by night. We may think this was a rare, even isolated, incident without particular significance except as a beacon to guide the way. The pillar, however, was a powerful manifestation of the Shechinah. When we understand that the Israelites were led not by a cloud, but by the Shechinah, which indicates the presence of the Lord, the impact of the event increases.

This fiery pillar is much more than a miraculous physical manifestation; it signifies the Lord's presence. When we understand its meaning, the Shechinah can become a fiery key to unlock our understanding of Christ and our covenants with him.

The idea of the Shechinah is not unknown among us. Look at a child's drawing of Jesus; it will probably show streams of light around his personage. This is the child's way of showing the glory of God, which is the Shechinah. We have all seen pictures showing great light from heaven, indicating the presence of the Lord. This, too, depicts the Shechinah.

We sing of it often in our hymns. For example, "Redeemer of Israel . . . Our shadow by day And our pillar by night" (*Hymns,* p. 6) is an obvious reference to appearances of the Shechinah, past and future.

As a caution, the word *Shechinah* should not be confused with a word that sounds similar—*kachina,* a Hopi Indian doll symbolizing a deified ancestral spirit.

What the Shechinah Is

The Shechinah is a manifestation of the presence of our true Lord, Jesus Christ. The LDS Bible dictionary says, "*Shechinah. The Presence.* A word used by the later Jews (and borrowed from them by the Christians) to denote the cloud of brightness and glory that marked the presence of the Lord." (p. 773.)

Smith's Bible Dictionary, a respected Christian source, elaborates on the Shechinah as a manifestation of the Divine Presence, "the idea which the different accounts in Scripture convey is that of a most brilliant and glorious light, enveloped in a cloud, and usually concealed by the cloud, so that the cloud itself was for the most part alone visible, but on particular occasions the glory appeared." (p. 631.)

Understanding the Shechinah can bring a new level of meaning to the scriptures. After learning about the Shechinah, my teenage son realized that Lehi had not merely seen "a pillar of fire . . . upon a rock before him," but that Christ had actually appeared to Lehi. (1 Nephi 1:6.) In much the same way, the Shechinah will open scriptures to new meaning for you.

Since the term *Shechinah* is Hebrew, the word is not used in our scriptures. The Shechinah itself, however, is all through our scriptures, expressed with a variety of words. We simply have to know what to watch for. Some common clue words are *brightness, cloud, fire, glory, light,* and *pillar of.*

Other less familiar words are *beryl, color of amber, polished brass, lamps, burning lamps, lightning,* and *smoking furnace.* Beryl, a hard mineral, occurs in colored or white prisms. Amber is a hard, yellowish, translucent resin that takes a fine polish. Brass, polished or burnished, gives the highest luster of any substance. In the King James Bible, polished brass is translated "amber" and signifies glory. (See *Old Testament: Student Manual, 1 Kings–Malachi,* p. 266.)

Taken together, the meanings of the substitute English words help us understand the powerful meaning *Shechinah* should have. We need to read these clue words carefully; sometimes these words are used as synonyms for *Shechinah* and sometimes not. Watch for indications of the Lord's presence. By recognizing the symbol and its meaning, we will read the scriptures with eyes that see. We will recognize Christ's presence among us, individually and as a people. We will know why he comes, and be ready when he comes again.

The Shechinah, the Jews, and the Latter-day Saints

The word *Shechinah* and its meaning are familiar to Jews, ancient and modern. The term first appeared in the ancient *Targum,* an ancient Aramaic language translation of the Old Testament that the Jews still use. Even today, references to the Shechinah are threaded through Hebrew traditions.

Because Latter-day Saints are of the House of Israel (mostly through Ephraim), we are entitled to understand the terminology and concept of the Shechinah. While the Jews know the word and the symbol, because of modern

revelation we have other insights into the glory of the
Lord. This book combines Hebrew and Latter-day Saint
teachings. By bringing together the physical symbol and
the spiritual significance of the Shechinah, we add
another dimension to our scripture reading and to our
spiritual lives.

The ancient Israelites saw the symbol of the Lord's
presence (physical aspect) but failed to recognize or honor
him as their God (spiritual application). Their lips said,
"The Lord, he is God," but their actions said, "The Lord he
is not our God." Rejecting him by their behavior, through
sin and rebellion, they became unworthy. Thus, the Lord
withdrew his presence as well as the ordinances of the temple he had come to bring them. As a result, the Israelites
failed to obtain what he had personally offered them—the
opportunity to dwell with him.

The Lord came in the meridian of time for the same
purpose—to teach man how to dwell with God. Again man
failed to recognize him. In our day he has come and continues to come, far more often than supposed, to show us how
to return and dwell with him.

When the Lord comes to claim his people and establish
his kingdom, will we be any different from the generations
preceding us? The sign of the Son of Man will herald his
coming. Will we recognize him and his sign, and, more
importantly, will we be prepared to dwell with him?

Learning of the Shechinah Helps us Prepare

The Shechinah is more than a pillar of fire in the
wilderness and more than a cloud filling the temple
of Solomon. The most obvious purpose of this physical manifestation is to witness of Jesus Christ and of
his presence among us. By studying the Shechinah,
we realize that the Lord's appearances and his work
center in his temples. As Nephi emphasized, "The

keeper of the gate [of heaven, or the temple] is the Holy One of Israel; and he employeth no servant there." (2 Nephi 9:41.) The Divine Presence illuminates the divine nature and mission of the temple.

This book, therefore, is about Jesus Christ, his work, and his glory. By learning to understand the symbolism of the Shechinah, we will comprehend that Christ's work and intent is for us to attain a glory like unto his own. We will see the Savior and ourselves in a new perspective and gain a greater appreciation of our covenant relationship with him. We will learn how to recognize the sign of the Son of Man proclaiming the arrival of the Second Coming. Understanding the Shechinah can set our spiritual lives ablaze and help us prepare to joyfully greet and live with the Savior.

2

EARLY COVENANTS OF THE LORD

A wonderful treasury of stories showing the Beloved Son of God interacting with man is stored in the Old Testament. In the beginning, the earth was created as a testing place where we could prove ourselves worthy to live with Heavenly Father eternally. Jehovah, who would later be Savior and Mediator, worked first as Creator of the earth, then as Tutor of its people. He taught Adam and Eve in person in the Garden of Eden and oversaw their education after they left his presence. Next, he privately instructed righteous men, who, because of their divine education, became prophets and taught mankind in his place. Motivated by love, he directed the earth's unfolding drama. He personally pursued an active role, "For behold," he said, "this is my work and my glory—to bring to pass the immortality and eternal life of man." (Moses 1:39.) The ultimate goal was to bring not a few people, but whole nations, back to his Father.

Adam, the first prophet, taught his children what the Lord had taught him. In spite of his teachings, his son Cain chose evil over good. The ability to choose whether or not to heed the Lord's prophets was a condition of earth life, and wickedness grew. Six generations from Adam (who still lived) a glorious success for the righteous occurred.

Enoch

The wonderful story of Enoch, only alluded to in Genesis, is recorded in the Pearl of Great Price. Humble Enoch, in spite of his stutter and the hatred of the people, built Zion in the midst of wickedness. His story is a prototype for us to follow.

One day as Enoch prayed, a voice told him to go to the mountain. He wrote, "I beheld the heavens open . . . And I saw the Lord; and he stood before my face, and he talked with me, even as a man talketh one with another, face to face." (Moses 7:3–4.)

During this glorious visit, Enoch was commanded to preach repentance. He obeyed, but his preaching offended men everywhere. They claimed, "A wild man hath come among us." (Moses 6:38.) Undaunted, Enoch preached, "All men, everywhere, must repent, or they can in nowise inherit the kingdom of God, for no unclean thing can dwell there, or dwell in his presence." (Moses 6:57.)

Through Enoch's persistence, many did repent. In time, the people divided. Among the wicked, wars and bloodshed raged continually. Among the repentant, however, "the Lord came and dwelt with his people, and they dwelt in righteousness." Moreover, "the fear of the Lord was upon all nations, so great was the glory of the Lord, which was upon his people." (Moses 7:16–17.)

This scripture illustrates two great consequences of Enoch's efforts. First, the Lord succeeded in establishing a people on earth among whom he could live. Second, the Shechinah, that is, the glory of the Lord, shone so brightly among his people that other nations, seeing it, were afraid. The sign became both a reward for righteousness and a protection from evil.

Enoch continued teaching the people of God and built a city called "the City of Holiness, even ZION." (Moses 7:19.) God talked with Enoch and showed him all the events from the time when Enoch's city would be "taken up into heaven" (Moses 7:21) to a time when there would be a new Zion, where "thou and all thy city [shall] meet them." (Moses 7:63.) In unity, "Enoch and all his people walked with God, and he dwelt in the midst of Zion; and it came to pass that Zion was not, for God received it up into his own bosom." (Moses 7:69.)

A noted gospel scholar, Sidney B. Sperry, commented, "When one thinks of Enoch and his people who walked with God and were received into his bosom, it seems incredible that they should be so received without the temple endowments usually given to men in holy temples only." (*Improvement Era*, November, 1955, p. 814.) When reflecting on the purpose of the temple covenants, and when reflecting on what happened to the City of Enoch, it stands to reason that the City of Enoch had temples.

Enoch's Zion is the only earthly society of which we are aware where the people were so righteous that the glorified Lord could dwell in their midst and personally minister to them. What a glorious example for us to follow. We will see the significance of this as the symbolism of the Shechinah unfolds.

Abraham

The God of the Old Testament made covenants with Abraham in person. First, Jehovah said, "I will make of thee a great nation." (Genesis 12:2.) When Abraham later complained that he was still childless, the Lord answered, "Look now toward heaven, and tell the stars, if thou be able to number them . . . So shall thy seed be." (Genesis 15:5.) During the same visit "the Lord made a covenant with Abram, saying, Unto thy seed have I given this land." (Genesis 15:18.)

Another lesser known but vitally important promise was, "I will establish my covenant between me and thee and thy seed after thee . . . to be a God unto thee." (Genesis 17:7.) On this covenant relationship hangs all the other promises, even for us today as part of Abraham's seed.

Isaac

The Lord appeared to Abraham's son, Isaac, offering the same promises. "I will make thy seed to multiply as the stars of heaven." (Genesis 26:4.)

Jacob

In a dream, Jacob, son of Isaac, saw a ladder reaching from earth to heaven. Above the ladder stood the Lord repeating the same covenants. Jacob responded, "Surely the LORD is in this place; and I knew it not . . . this is none other but the house of God, and this is the gate of heaven." (Genesis 28:16–17. *The Old Testament Student Manual, Genesis–2 Samuel,* p. 86, discusses covenants as rungs on a ladder.) Jacob changed the name of the place to Beth-el, meaning "house of God." Many years later, God told him to return to Beth-el and to make an altar. There God appeared to him a second time, changing his name to Israel and renewing the promises of land and posterity.

Joseph

From there, the story took a strange and interesting twist. Through a series of events, the covenant family

left behind the land of inheritance and moved into idol-
atrous Egypt. At a time and place unknown to us,
Joseph, one of the twelve sons of Jacob, received the
"blessings of [his] father." (Genesis 49:26.) When the
covenant family arrived in Egypt, it consisted of only
seventy people. Not yet did they number as the stars,
nor were they strong enough to battle for and claim
their promised lands. After Joseph died, all his family
and posterity were put under bondage as aliens in a for-
eign land.

Long before the Israelites became slaves, the Lord
told Abraham, "Know of a surety that thy seed shall be
a stranger in a land that is not theirs, and shall serve
them; and they shall afflict them four hundred years."
(Genesis 15:13.) However, it was through their bondage
that the Israelites were preserved, for Egypt was a cra-
dle of peace whereas their own lands were a battlefield.
Slavery, which isolated them socially, also preserved
their national identity because they married among
themselves. In Canaan far too many would have polluted the lineage by marrying outside the covenant.
Four hundred years later, Pharaoh worried about the
size of the Israelite multitude, indicating that the Lord's
plan was a success. The Lord had his people, with lineage intact, ready to claim the temporal blessing of the
lands promised them. His intent was also to prepare
them for, and present them with, the more important
spiritual blessings inherent in the promises given to the
fathers.

As we study the scriptural account of the chosen
people, we shall learn what the Lord intended to
give. What he intended for them, he also wants for
us. As the seed of Abraham, we are heirs to the
same spiritual promises.

3

THE SHECHINAH AND THE CHILDREN OF ISRAEL

The Shechinah Appears

We remember the story of exiled Moses tending sheep near mount Sinai. Unexpectedly, the "presence of the Lord appeared unto him in a flame of fire out of the midst of a bush; and . . . the bush burned with fire, and the bush was not consumed." (JST, Exodus 3:2.) When the Lord announced his identity, Moses "hid his face; for he was afraid to look upon God." (Exodus 3:6.) The Lord then commissioned him to bring the children of Israel out of Egypt.

Moses knew it was one thing to witness an incredible event himself, but quite another to convince others that he had seen it. "They will not believe me," he protested. "They will say, The LORD hath not appeared unto thee." (Exodus 4:1.) The Lord showed Moses three signs to convince the people; when Moses performed these signs in Egypt, the Israelites believed. When Moses wrote of seeing the burning bush and the "presence of the Lord . . . in a flame of fire," he was describing the Shechinah. Although the Lord had appeared previously many times, this was the first obvious recorded incidence of a fiery accompaniment. (See Genesis 15:17–18 for an obscure earlier reference.) As we shall see, this manifestation, given at the outset of Moses' mission, was an indication that the Lord intended to go with Moses to claim his people and to be their God.

On another occasion before starting his mission, Moses talked face to face with God. God offered to show Moses his works, "but not all," because "no man can behold all my works, except he behold all my glory; and no man can behold all my glory, and afterwards remain in the flesh on the earth." (Moses 1:4, 5.) This scripture teaches that the full glory of God is too much for mortal man to witness. The Shechinah, therefore, is more like a sign revealing a portion of his glory.

After the Lord's departure, Satan appeared to Moses, but Moses could easily see the difference between the two visitors, for Satan had no glory. "This one God only will I worship," Moses affirmed, "which is the God of glory." (Moses 1:20.) When Satan departed, Moses called upon God and "beheld his glory again." (Moses 1:25.) These back-to-back appearances teach us that the glorious light surrounding God is discernible, physical, and real.

Following the Lord's instructions, Moses petitioned the Egyptian government to let the Israelites go. The plagues on Egypt, some of them foreshadowing future events, were caused by Pharaoh's disobedience to the divine decree. After the death of the firstborn males, symbolic of Christ's future sacrifice to free us all from the bondage of sin, Pharaoh, in desperation, told Moses and his people to "be gone." (Exodus 12:32.)

Once the children of Israel arrived at the edge of the wilderness, the Lord "went before them by day in a pillar of a cloud, to lead them the way; and by night in a pillar of fire, to give them light; to go by day and night. He took not away the pillar of the cloud by day, nor the pillar of fire by night, from before the people" (Exodus 13:21–22.)

The cloud by day and the pillar of fire by night
are one and the same thing—the manifestation of
the Divine Presence. It dwelt with the Israelites continually. In the daytime, a cloud was visible, much
like a screen, surrounding the light within. In the
darkness of night, the fire within the cloud glowed
through. Thus did all the hosts of Israel first see the
Shechinah.

The Shechinah and a Covenant People

Let us now refer more specifically to the scriptures so we can more readily see the Shechinah "in
action" and realize for ourselves how constantly it
appeared to oversee the affairs of the children of
Israel. Regardless of the differing English terminology
used to describe or indicate the Shechinah, it is the
presence of the Lord Jesus Christ to which we are
referring. We can thereby watch him at work, striving to prepare a people to dwell with him.

After the children of Israel escaped from Egypt,
Pharaoh changed his mind yet again and sent his
entire army to recapture them. At this point the "pillar of the cloud went from before their face, and stood
behind them: And it came between the camp of the
Egyptians and the camp of Israel; and it was a cloud
and darkness to them [the Egyptians], but it gave
light by night." (Exodus 14:19–20.)

The strategic relocation of the pillar made it obvious to the Israelite's that, as Moses had told them,
"The LORD shall fight for you." (Exodus 14:14.) While
the pillar stood guard, the wind made a dry highway
between walls of water across the Red Sea. The
Israelites fled across; the Egyptians pursued. But "in
the morning watch the LORD looked unto the host of
the Egyptians through the pillar of fire and of the

cloud." (Exodus 14:24.) Clearly, the Lord was inside the pillar. Next, he caused the Egyptian's chariot wheels to drag heavily in the sea-bottom. Recognizing the power against them, the Egyptians said, "The LORD fighteth for them [Israel] against the Egyptians." (Exodus 14:25.) But it was too late to flee. The Egyptians drowned in the churning water as the sea returned to normal. Because of this miracle, the people believed in the Lord. The Lord, not a mysterious fire, had saved them.

Seeing their rescue, the camp of Israel sang of victory: "Thou shalt bring [thy people] in, and plant them in the mountain of thine inheritance, in the place, O LORD, which thou hast made for thee to dwell in, in the Sanctuary, O Lord." (Exodus 15:17.) Thus (as though they understood) the people sang of their God leading them to where they might dwell with him.

Their exultation was short-lived, however. Traveling into the desert, the Israelites found no water for three days. When they did find it, the water was bitter, and they complained. The Lord, in his kindness showed Moses how to sweeten it. Soon, they complained of hunger, and the Lord sent manna. The Lord would sustain them with the bread and water of life even as he prepared them for the feast of spiritual life.

Not long after these events, Moses informed the people, "In the morning . . . ye shall see the glory of the LORD." (Exodus 16:7.) They needed to prepare and repent from their murmurings. The next morning as Aaron spoke to all the people, they "looked toward the wilderness [where they had last seen the Shechinah], and, behold, the glory of the LORD appeared in the cloud." (Exodus 16:10.) The people saw that the Divine Presence was watching over them yet.

The Covenant People Meet the Lord

After three months of troubles and travels, the Israelites pitched camp at the base of mount Sinai in the desert. The people promised the Lord, through Moses, "All that the LORD hath spoken we will do." (Exodus 19:8.) Moses took their message back to the Lord, whereupon the Lord promised, "Lo, I come unto thee in a thick cloud, that the people may hear when I speak with thee, and believe thee for ever." (Exodus 19:9.)

To hear the voice of the Lord was even greater than to see the Shechinah, and the people had to purify themselves. They were warned that they must not enter or touch the mountain. In the morning, after three days of preparation, there were "thunders and lightnings, and a thick cloud upon the mount," causing the people to tremble. (Exodus 19:16.) Moses brought the people to the foot of the mountain to meet their God. "And mount Sinai was altogether on a smoke, because the LORD descended upon it in fire: and the smoke thereof ascended as the smoke of a furnace, and the whole mount quaked greatly." (Exodus 19:18.) Generations later the psalmist retold the visitation at Sinai: "The earth shook, the heavens also dropped at the presence of God: even Sinai itself was moved at the presence of God, the God of Israel." (Psalms 68:8.)

The people were again warned that to enter the mount would bring certain death, but Moses and Aaron were allowed to approach. Then God spoke the ten commandments plainly for all to hear. "And all the people saw the thunderings, and the lightnings, and the noise of the trumpet, and the mountain smoking: and when the people saw it, they removed, and stood afar off." (Exodus 20:18.)

They were so frightened by this experience that they begged Moses, "Speak thou with us, and we will

hear; but let not God speak with us, lest we die."
(Exodus 20:19.) Moses reassured them, saying, in
essence, that God wanted them to revere him always
so they would not sin. By hearing his voice they could
not doubt his godhood nor his reality. While the people stood apart, shaken from their experience, the
Lord impressed upon them, "Ye have seen that I
have talked with you from heaven." (Exodus 20:22.)
He did not want them to forget him. In response,
the congregation covenanted to do "all the words
which the LORD hath said." (Exodus 24:3.)

Next, a rare and significant event occurred.
Moses, Aaron, Nadab and Abihu (Aaron's sons), and
seventy of the elders of Israel climbed mount Sinai.
All seventy-four "saw the God of Israel." They
reported that "there was under his feet as it were a
paved work of a sapphire stone, and as it were the
body of heaven in his clearness." (Exodus 24:10.)
Confirming the truth, the scripture re-emphasized,
"also they saw God." (Exodus 24:11.)

Four simple, easily-missed words reported what
transpired inside the cloud. The God of Israel and
his guests "did eat and drink." (Exodus 24:11.) In a
parallel event, the God of the New Testament ate
and drank with his invited guests. That meal, the
Last Supper, established a covenant between the
living God and his people. This same Jesus Christ,
as God of the Old Testament, dined with mortal
guests on mount Sinai. This, too, was a covenant
meal uniting God and man. In fact, one probable
root for the word *covenant* means "to eat bread
with." (See Victor L. Ludlow, "Unlocking Old Testament Prophecy," *Ensign,* October, 1990, p. 60.)

When we partake of the sacrament today, we
"eat and drink" with the Lord. Our reverence for
the sacrament deepens when we think of it as a
covenant meal with him. Actually, the sacrament is

a *type* which foreshadows a future time when we
will sit down personally with the Covenant Giver
at our own covenant meal. (See D&C 27:5, 14.)
Conceivably, the experience of the group on mount
Sinai was also a type of this promised future event.

The Offer

Soon after making oral covenants, the Lord
asked Moses to enter the mount to receive a written law. When Moses went up, a "cloud covered the
mount. And the glory of the LORD abode upon
mount Sinai, and the cloud covered it six days: and
the seventh day he called unto Moses out of the
midst of the cloud. And the sight of the glory of the
LORD was like devouring fire on the top of the
mount in the eyes of the children of Israel. And
Moses went into the midst of the cloud, and . . .
was in the mount forty days and forty nights."
(Exodus 24:15–18.)

The Lord revealed to Moses his divine intention.
He told Moses to have the people contribute materials and labor, and "make me a sanctuary [temple];
that I may dwell among them." (Exodus 25:8.) He
promised, "And there I will meet with thee, and I
will commune with thee from above the mercy
seat." (Exodus 25:22.) This meeting was spiritually
essential for the Israelites because the mercy seat
represented atonement. Jehovah added, "I will
meet with the children of Israel, and the tabernacle
shall be sanctified by my glory [presence]. And I
will sanctify the tabernacle of the congregation. . . .
And I will dwell among the children of Israel, and
will be their God. And they shall know that I am
the LORD their God, that brought them forth out of
the land of Egypt, that I may dwell among them: I
am the LORD their God." (Exodus 29:43–46.)

The Sign of the Sabbath

Just before issuing the written law, the Lord gave Moses a final, crucial instruction. Teach the people, the Lord stressed, that "my sabbaths ye shall keep: for it is a sign between me and you throughout your generations; that ye may know that I am the LORD that doth sanctify you." In typical Hebrew style he repeated, "Wherefore the children of Israel shall keep the sabbath, to observe the sabbath throughout their generations, for a perpetual covenant. It is a sign between me and the children of Israel for ever." (Exodus 31:13, 16–17.) Thus, keeping the Sabbath was, and still is, a sign of belonging to the covenant people.

We have read how the Lord wanted a sanctuary built and how the tabernacle would be sanctified by him. Now he said he would sanctify the people. It becomes clear, then, that the tabernacle was a place where the Lord would sanctify his people.

During the forty days Moses received instruction from the Lord, the Shechinah glowed over the holy mount. In parting, the Lord gave Moses "two tables of testimony, tables of stone, written with the finger of God." (Exodus 31:18.) Here was the instruction manual, straight from the Inventor, on how to become sanctified.

Jehovah had now made two great promises to the children of Israel: to dwell with them, and to sanctify them. The Shechinah became the symbol of these proffered blessings.

4

THE SHECHINAH
IN THE WILDERNESS

A Stiff-Necked People

While Moses received divine instruction, the people
sinned by making and worshiping the golden calf.
Even as they did so, they could plainly see the Shechinah, which testified of the presence of the Lord.

At the same time, the Lord could see them, and he
was angered at what he saw. "Let me alone," he told
Moses, "that my wrath may wax hot against them,
and that I may consume them." (Exodus 32:10.)
Moses tried to intervene. "Turn from thy fierce
wrath," he pleaded. "Thy people will repent of this
evil." (JST, Exodus 32:12.)

Moses departed the mount carrying the two
tables, written on both sides, which were the work of
God. When he came in view of the camp, Moses saw
for himself the scene the Lord had described. Now
Moses' anger "waxed hot," and he threw the tables
and broke them. His action symbolized a broken
covenant which carried serious consequence. As an
immediate punishment for their sins, three thousand
guilty men were slain by the sons of Levi that day.
The next day Moses returned to the Lord, hoping to
reconcile the people. The Lord held each individual
accountable, saying, "Whosoever hath sinned against
me, him will I blot out of my book." (Exodus 32:33.)

In addition, as a group the people lost an enormous blessing: the Lord refused to go before them into battle. Instead, he decreed, "I will send an angel before thee . . . for I will not go up in the midst of thee; for thou art a stiffnecked people: lest I consume thee in the way." (Exodus 33:2–3.) When the people heard, they mourned.

Reconciliation

Moses took one of his own tents and pitched it outside the camp as a place to seek the Lord. When Moses first went there, every man eagerly stood at his own tent door, watching. As Moses entered, the "cloudy pillar descended, and stood at the door of the tabernacle, and the LORD talked with Moses. And all the people saw the cloudy pillar stand at the tabernacle door: and all the people rose up and worshipped, every man in his tent door. And the LORD spake unto Moses face to face, as a man speaketh unto his friend." (Exodus 33:9–11.) The people worshiped because they knew from the sign of the cloud that the Lord was there, and they hoped to appease his anger.

However, the critical meeting occurred when Moses went back to the mountain to ask forgiveness for his people after their sin. We can hardly imagine the preparation and trepidation with which Moses must have approached the Lord. By facing the personal wrath of God to mediate for the people, Moses jeopardized his own standing. Yet, Christlike, he interceded. Moses pleaded that the Lord still consider them his people. The Lord relented, "My presence shall go with thee." (Exodus 33:14.) Moses pressed, "Wherein shall it be known here that I and thy people have found grace in thy sight? is it not in that thou goest with us?" (Exodus 33:16.) The Lord answered, "I will do this thing." (Exodus 33:17.)

Seeking further reconciliation, Moses beseeched, "Shew me thy glory." (Exodus 33:18.) The Lord agreed, with a limitation. "Thou canst not see my face at this time, lest mine anger be kindled against thee also, and I destroy thee, and thy people." (JST, Exodus 33:20.) The Lord instructed Moses where to stand "while my glory passeth by," saying, "[I] will cover thee with my hand while I pass by; And I will take away mine hand, and thou shalt see my back parts; but my face shall not be seen as at other times; for I am angry with my people Israel." (JST, Exodus 33:22–23.)

Through courage and great humility, Moses won another opportunity for Israel. With the Lord's mercy and help, he would start anew to build a righteous nation. Isaiah later wrote of Jehovah's mercy, "In his love and in his pity he redeemed them; and he bare them, and carried them all the days of old." (Isaiah 63:9.)

Moses returned the next morning to mount Sinai, where "the Lord descended in the cloud, and stood with him there." (Exodus 34:5.) Moses worshiped before the Lord and again petitioned for the covenant inheritance. The Lord answered, "Behold, I make a covenant." (Exodus 34:10.) Moses then spent another forty days with the Lord and returned to the people with a second set of tables, which were nearly the same as the first.

The Shechinah and the Tabernacle

After receiving the second set of stone tables, a willing and generous people began preparing the tabernacle. Because all the work was done as commanded, Moses blessed the people. On the first day of the second year, the day appointed by the Lord, the tabernacle was raised and the contents placed inside. Moses washed the hands and feet of Aaron and his sons. "Then a cloud covered the tent of the congregation, and the glory of the LORD filled the tabernacle. And Moses was not able to enter into the tent of the congregation, because the cloud abode thereon, and the glory of the LORD filled the tabernacle." (Exodus 40:34–35.)

A parallel account in Numbers reads, "And on the day that the tabernacle was reared up the cloud covered the tabernacle, namely, the tent of the testimony: and at even there was upon the tabernacle as it were the appearance of fire, until the morning." (Numbers 9:15.)

On the eighth day of preparatory ceremonies, the people drew near to the tabernacle, and Moses instructed, "This is the thing which the LORD commanded that ye should do: and the glory of the LORD shall appear unto you." (Leviticus 9:6.) The people understood that its appearance would indicate both the Divine Presence and divine approval. After completing specific requirements, Moses and Aaron "blessed the people: and the glory of the LORD appeared unto all the people. And there came a fire out from before the LORD, and consumed upon the altar the burnt offering and the fat: which when all the people saw, they shouted, and fell on their faces." (Leviticus 9:23–24.) Not only did the glory, or Shechinah, come, but fire from the Lord consumed their sacrifice.

Before long, Nadab and Abihu, who were priests and sons of Aaron, offered "strange fire" in the tabernacle, which was forbidden. Consequently, "there went out fire from the LORD, and devoured them, and they died before the LORD." (Leviticus 10:1–2.) Thus the people learned that the fire of the Lord blessed or destroyed according to their worthiness. This same dual role will appear again in the last days, when fire from the Lord will destroy the wicked and cleanse the earth for the righteous.

That the Lord would commune from the mercy seat had been promised before the tabernacle was built. Moses had access to the holiest place, for when he went to speak with the Lord, he heard "one speaking unto him from off the mercy seat that was upon the ark of testimony, from between the two cherubims." (Numbers 7:89.) However, the Lord, through Moses, warned Aaron not to enter the innermost chamber, which held the mercy seat, so that "he die not: for I will appear in the cloud upon the mercy seat." (Leviticus 16:2.) Moses could physically withstand the Lord's presence, but Aaron could not.

The Lord commanded the Israelites, "I am the LORD your God . . . ye shall be holy." (Leviticus 11:44.) If they kept his commandments, he offered them many wonderful blessings. In words once spoken to Abraham, he promised, "I will . . . establish my covenant with you." (Leviticus 26:9.) The ultimate blessing, once achieved by Enoch, was, "I will walk among you, and will be your God, and ye shall be my people." (Leviticus 26:12.) This blessing was foreshadowed by the Shechinah resting day and night upon the tabernacle. In a sense, the Shechinah was both a promise and a fulfillment.

The Shechinah as a Guide

The book of Exodus clearly shows the Shechinah's role as a guide to the children of Israel in their travels. "When the cloud was taken up from over the tabernacle, the children of Israel went onward in all their journeys: But if the cloud were not taken up, then they journeyed not till the day that it was taken up. For the cloud of the LORD was upon the tabernacle by day, and fire was on it by night, in the sight of all the house of Israel, throughout all their journeys." (Exodus 40:36–38; see also Numbers 9:16–22.) About two months after erecting the tabernacle, "the cloud was taken up from off the tabernacle. . . . And the children of Israel took their journeys out of the wilderness of Sinai; and the cloud rested in the wilderness of Paran." (Numbers 10:11–12.) When Moses and his father-in-law went "to search out a resting place, . . . the cloud of the LORD was upon them." (Numbers 10:33–34.)

A Fire That Consumed

Although the Lord was leading and caring for the people, they complained. This "displeased the Lord [who] heard it; and his anger was kindled; and the fire of the LORD burnt among them, and consumed them." Ingratitude toward the Lord merited a serious penalty. Extremely frightened, the people "cried unto Moses; and when Moses prayed unto the LORD, the fire was quenched." They named the place "Taberah: because the fire of the LORD burnt among them." (Numbers 11:1–3.)

The Shechinah and the Leaders

Because the responsibility of leadership for the multitude weighed heavily on Moses, the Lord told him to gather seventy elders at the tabernacle, and he would "come down and talk" with them. (Numbers 11:17.) When they assembled, "the LORD came down in a cloud, and spake unto him, and took of the spirit that was upon him, and gave it unto the seventy elders," thereby sharing the burden. (Numbers 11:25.) Thus these seventy (perhaps the same group who had eaten with the Lord on the mount) received their authority personally from the Lord.

The Lord appeared again when Moses' own brother and sister complained against him. Calling to Moses,

Aaron, and Miriam, the Lord commanded sternly, "Come out ye three unto the tabernacle of the congregation." They hurried to obey because they recognized his voice. "And the LORD came down in the pillar of the cloud, and stood in the door of the tabernacle." (Numbers 12:4–5.) In anger the Lord chastised Aaron and Miriam, and when he departed "the cloud departed from off the tabernacle." (Numbers 12:10.) By their complaining, Aaron and Miriam caused the entire multitude to lose the presence of the Lord for a time.

Rebellion and a Lost Inheritance

Trouble arose again after twelve spies returned from surveying the promised land. Afraid of the inhabitants, ten of them were ready to return to Egypt. Only Joshua and Caleb gave a good report of the promised land. The people, rebelling at their report, became angry and determined to stone them. But "the glory of the LORD appeared . . . before all the children of Israel." (Numbers 14:10.) The Lord, in protecting Joshua and Caleb, was also ready to smite and disinherit the unrighteous.

Moses interceded, saying, "[the Egyptians] have heard that thou LORD art among this people, that thou LORD art seen face to face, and that thy cloud standeth over them, and that thou goest before them, by day time in a pillar of a cloud, and in a pillar of fire by night." (Numbers 14:14.) If the people are destroyed, Moses argued, the news will spread that the Lord slew them because he was incapable of bringing them into the land as he promised. Because Moses pleaded for mercy, the Lord pardoned the people. "But," he added, "as truly as I live, all the earth shall be filled with the glory of the LORD." (Numbers 14:21.)

The Lord seemed to be saying, "In spite of you, the earth shall yet be filled with my glory." The Lord had intended to dwell with his people in their promised land. From there his glory could spread and fill the earth, but Israel's rebellion made such fulfillment impossible at this time. The declaration "as truly as I live" sealed an oath.

The Lord pronounced a dire consequence for the rebellion. "All those men which have seen my glory, and my miracles . . . and have not hearkened to my voice . . . shall not see the land which I sware unto their fathers, neither shall any of them that provoked me see it." (Numbers 14:22–23.) This decree barred all unworthy adults from the promised land.

With such a punishment, some of the rebellious suddenly decided they wanted to enter the promised land after all. Moses warned them that the Lord would not go with them, but they went anyway. The inhabitants of the area they invaded promptly killed them. Obedience was the prerequisite for the Lord to go before them; without him, they could not be victorious in battle.

Such a drastic lesson should have proved that the Lord was in charge. But before long, another rebellion challenged Moses' leadership. Korah, the ringleader, gathered all the congregation against him at the tabernacle door. The Lord confronted the mutiny personally, for "the glory of the LORD appeared unto all the congregation." (Numbers 16:19.) The Lord took charge, and the "earth opened her mouth, and swallowed" Korah and his two cohorts. (Numbers 16:32.) As for the 250 men who had usurped priestly duties, "a fire from the Lord" came and consumed them. (Numbers 16:35.) It was clear that not following the Lord's appointed leader was the same as disobeying the Lord himself.

The Lord kept trying to get the people to "remember, and do all my commandments . . . [for] I am the LORD your God, which brought you out of the land of

Egypt, to be your God: I am the LORD your God."
(Numbers 15:40–41.) The fiery Shechinah over the
tabernacle was a visible reminder of that truth.

Though we do not currently see a cloud by day
and a pillar of fire by night, we must also remember
and keep all the Lord's commandments. An entire
generation of the children of Israel lost their
intended blessing—the inheritance of the promised
land where they would dwell with the Lord in his
glory. Through our actions, we will either lose or gain
this same blessing.

Moses' Farewell

After forty years of wandering, Moses gathered
the new generation of his people together and gave
them detailed instructions. In three intensive sermons, he recounted the Lord's personal dealings
among them, referring frequently to the Shechinah
to prove the Lord's presence and power. "[He] went in
the way before you, to search you out a place to pitch
your tents in, in fire by night, to shew you by what
way ye should go, and in a cloud by day," Moses
began. (Deuteronomy 1:33.)

As children they had stood near a mountain that
had "burned with fire unto the midst of heaven, with
darkness, clouds, and thick darkness." Moses reminded
them that "The LORD spake unto you out of the midst of
the fire: ye heard the voice of the words, . . . out of the
midst of the fire." (Deuteronomy 4:11-12, 15.)

"Take heed . . . lest ye forget the covenant of the
LORD," Moses warned, "for the LORD thy God is a consuming fire, even a jealous God." (Deuteronomy 4:23–24.)
There are rewards for remembering, Moses assured
them. "If thou seek him with all thy heart and with all
thy soul . . . he will not forsake thee . . . nor forget the
covenant of thy fathers." (Deuteronomy 4:29, 31.)

As proof of the Lord's goodness to them in the future, Moses cited his favor to them in the recent past. Of all earth's people, he insisted, none had experienced anything as great as this: "Did ever people hear the voice of God speaking out of the midst of the fire, as thou hast heard, and live?" (Deuteronomy 4:33.) The reason for this experience was "that thou mightest know that the LORD he is God; there is none else beside him." (Deuteronomy 4:35.) Moses repeated for emphasis, "Out of heaven he made thee to hear his voice, that he might instruct thee: and upon earth he shewed thee his great fire; and thou heardest his words out of the midst of the fire. . . . Know therefore . . . that the LORD he is God in heaven above." (Deuteronomy 4:36, 39.)

Later that month Moses again gathered Israel together, admonishing them to keep the commandments and to remember that the "LORD talked with you face to face in the mount out of the midst of the fire, (I stood between the LORD and you at that time, to shew you the word of the LORD: for ye were afraid by reason of the fire.)" (Deuteronomy 5:4–5.)

Moses then repeated the ten commandments. "These words," Moses stressed, "the LORD spake . . . out of the midst of the fire, of the cloud, and of the thick darkness, with a great voice: . . . And he wrote them in two tables of stone, and delivered them unto me. . . . And ye said, Behold the LORD our God hath shewed us his glory and his greatness, and we have heard his voice out of the midst of the fire: we have seen this day that God doth talk with man, and he liveth." (Deuteronomy 5:22, 24.) That God audibly spoke to man was conclusive proof that God lived

Moses reminded the people of their fear that "this great fire will consume us: if we hear the voice of the LORD our God any more, then we shall die. For who is there of all flesh, that hath heard the voice of the living God speaking out of the midst of the fire, as we

have, and lived?" (Deuteronomy 5:25–26.) Thus
Moses used a memory of their own fear as a testimony of the reality of their experience.

Moses counseled, "Ye shall walk in all the ways
which the LORD your God hath commanded you, that
ye may live, and that it may be well with you."
(Deuteronomy 5:33.) He was speaking here of physical life, with the days of battle yet ahead of them, but
he also meant spiritual life.

On the day Israel was to cross Jordan, Moses
spoke stressing again "the words, which the LORD
spake with you in the mount out of the midst of the
fire in the day of the assembly." (Deuteronomy 9:10.)
Knowing that many of the people had not then been
born, Moses added, "So I turned and came down from
the mount, and the mount burned with fire, and the
two tables of the covenant were in my two hands."
(Deuteronomy 9:15.)

Moses also specified regulations of cleanliness for
the people which were necessary to prepare the camp
for the Lord's presence. These were mandated
because "the LORD thy God walketh in the midst of
thy camp, to deliver thee, and to give up thine enemies before thee; therefore shall thy camp be holy."
(Deuteronomy 23:14.) If the people would obey, the
promise was: "I will walk among you, and will be your
God, and ye shall be my people." (Leviticus 26:12.)
The psalmist later celebrated the safety of this condition. "God is in the midst of her [Israel]; she shall not
be moved." (Psalms 46:5.)

During this final month of preparation before entering
the promised land, Moses tried to verbally shake the children of Israel into spiritual readiness. He revived the emo-
tions of what they had previously seen and heard and felt.
His urgent message stressed that the people had witnessed
undeniable, fiery proof that the living God was there, and
that they had better keep their covenants with him.

When Moses finished his instructions, the Lord told him to call Joshua before the people "that I may give him a charge. . . . And the LORD appeared in the tabernacle in a pillar of a cloud: and the pillar of the cloud stood over the door of the tabernacle." (Deuteronomy 31:14–15.) This appearance of the Shechinah verified that the Lord was with them yet. It also verified Joshua as the rightful leader. Shortly after this, Moses was taken by the Lord, and it was written, "there arose not a prophet since in Israel like unto Moses, whom the LORD knew face to face." (Deuteronomy 34:10.)

We who have not seen the Shechinah personally can believe Moses' words that he and all the children of Israel saw it. We can know that it indicated the actual presence of the Lord. We can apply Moses' admonitions to ourselves, for we too must walk in all the ways of the Lord and keep our covenants. Then the Lord will be with us, and it will be well with us.

THE SHECHINAH IN THE PROMISED LAND

When the children of Israel entered the promised land, the Lord covenanted to be with Joshua as he had been with Moses. (Joshua 3:7.) However, except for his ordination, not one incidence of the Shechinah was recorded during Joshua's judgment. It is sad to contrast these silent years with the fiery era of Moses, especially since the Lord intended to dwell with the people in their restored inheritance.

The period of judges, lasting approximately 350 years, generally lacked spirituality. However, when righteous Gideon was visited by an angel he offered a sacrifice, and the angel touched it with his staff. Suddenly "there rose up fire out of the rock, and consumed the flesh and the unleavened cakes." (Judges 6:21.) This was the same fire of the Lord which had consumed the first sacrifice in the tabernacle.

The Tabernacle Preserved

In spite of rampant apostasy, the tabernacle survived. Joshua erected it in Shiloh. Here, much later, the Lord "came, and stood" and called to young Samuel. (1 Samuel 3:10.) The tabernacle was used for more than 400 years. Solomon went to "Gibeon; for there was the tabernacle . . . which

Moses the servant of the LORD had made in the wilderness." (2 Chronicles 1:3.) When, why, or how it was moved to Gibeon (south of Shiloh and closer to Jerusalem), we have no record. By this time, the tabernacle was presided over by the priests, not by the fiery Divine Presence as in its glorious beginning.

The Loss of the Ark and the Glory of the Lord

The devastating loss of the presence of the Lord began with an unrighteous attempt to gain the protection of the Lord. Before Saul became king, the Israelite army was badly beaten by the Philistines. In fear, the survivors sent desperate word to Shiloh. Two priests (sons of Eli) removed the ark of the covenant from the tabernacle and carried it to the battle camp. The idea was to lead with it into battle so that the Lord would "go before them." The Philistines also understood the sacredness of the ark of the covenant, for they promptly moaned, "Woe unto us! who shall deliver us? . . . these are the Gods that smote the Egyptians." (1 Samuel 4:8.) However, the Israelites could not use unrighteous means to receive righteous favor, and thirty thousand of them were slaughtered. The two priests were also slain, and worst of all, the ark of the covenant was captured by the Philistines.

Dire consequences followed. The priest's widow grieved, not only for her dead husband, but more for the loss of the Lord's presence. She mourned, "The glory is departed from Israel: for the ark of God is taken." (1 Samuel 4:22.) The psalmist bemoaned the reality of this loss. "He forsook the tabernacle . . . And delivered his strength into captivity, and his glory into the enemy's hand." (Psalms 78:60.) The ultimate end of Israel's forsaking the Lord was that he forsook them.

It is essential to understand that the presence of the ark of the covenant and the presence of the Lord were inextricably linked. To remove the one meant to lose the other. The loss of the ark was shattering because it was the mercy seat, the place where man and God met and atonement occurred. Without God's mercy, man had no salvation. Yet, the Israelites foolishly risked and lost the mercy seat.

Because the Philistines did not know what to do with the ark of God, they put it into the house of Dagon, their idol god, setting the sacred object beside the profane. The next morning the idol was on the ground prostrate before the ark of the Lord; the second day it was again face down, but this time broken. This was only the beginning of trouble for the Philistines. For seven months they moved the ark from city to city, but afflictions followed it where ever it went. Finally they returned the ark to the Israelites, glad to be rid of it.

A Substitute King

About this time the people begged Samuel for a king. After the unholy removal of the throne of God from the tabernacle, it is no wonder the Lord told Samuel to comply, "for . . . they have rejected me, that I should not reign over them." (1 Samuel 8:7.) Shortly thereafter, Saul was crowned.

When David became king forty years later, the ark of the covenant had not been restored to its rightful place but sat in a house, forgotten by most of the people. David proposed moving it to Jerusalem, "for we enquired not at it in the days of Saul." (1 Chronicles 13:3.) They had not petitioned the Lord at the mercy seat in forty years—what a sad commentary on the state of Israel.

So David victoriously gathered Israel and, after
one unsuccessful try, carried out the ark of God in
rejoicing. The Levites carried the ark of God on their
shoulders with staves fitting through rings, which
allowed them to carry it without touching it. With
joyous music, the Israelites brought the ark of the
covenant to Jerusalem and into the prepared place, a
pitched tent.

Even though the tabernacle still existed, David
chose not to return the ark of the covenant to it. In
fact, the ark of the covenant never was returned to
the tabernacle. Instead, priests ministered in both
places.

David offered to build a permanent home for the
throne of God, but the Lord, through Nathan the
prophet, foretold that a son of David should build it.
Thus the ark of the covenant sat without glory in a
substitute tent, waiting the time of Solomon.

The Temple of Solomon

Solomon honored his father's charge to build "the
sanctuary" in order to "bring the ark of the covenant
of the LORD" into it. (1 Chronicles 22:19.) The site was
no ordinary one, for Solomon built "at Jerusalem in
mount Moriah, where the LORD appeared unto David
his father," the same mount where Abraham offered
Isaac. (2 Chronicles 3:1; see also Genesis 22:2.) This
site is even more significant today, for it will yet
house what the Jews call the Third Temple.

Speaking to Solomon, the Lord said, "Concerning
this house which thou art in building, if thou wilt . . .
keep all my commandments to walk in them; then . . .
I will dwell among the children of Israel, and will not
forsake my people Israel." (1 Kings 6:12–13.) This
was the promise given in the wilderness, now
renewed. That the Lord could dwell among the chil-

dren of Israel was possible yet. It was not a coinci-
dence that the offer came when the temple was built.
Temples and promises go together; when temples are
constructed, promises become possible. This was true
with the tabernacle and with Solomon's temple, and
it remains true for us today.

The temple, finished in seven years, was far from
ordinary. Solomon beautified the temple with precious gems and gold. The altar in the Holy of Holies
was overlaid with gold, as were the cherubim. All the
vessels were pure gold. The doors and the floor were
overlaid with gold. Even the nails were gold.

The Hebrew word for *temple* is nearly equiva-
lent to the English word *palace*. (LDS Bible Dictionary, p. 782.) Indeed, the splendid temple was a
suitable home for the throne of God. As a final
preparation, the Levites brought the throne, the
all-important mercy seat, from its temporary tabernacle, into the Holy of Holies and left it under
guard of the cherubim. There they drew out the
staves of the ark, an act which represented its per-
manence in the house of God. The only thing inside
the ark was the covenant—the two tables of stone
written on at Sinai. Written on enduring stone, the
covenant between the Lord and the children of
Israel likewise still endured.

The Shechinah Returned

When the priests came out of the Holy of Holies,
the "trumpeters and singers were as one . . . and
when they . . . praised the LORD, . . . the house was
filled with a cloud, even the house of the LORD; So
that the priests could not stand to minister by reason
of the cloud: for the glory of the LORD had filled the
house of God." (2 Chronicles 5:13–14; see also 1 Kings
8:10–11.)

What a glorious manifestation of divine approval. The Shechinah had returned. Solomon recognized the Shechinah for he said, "The LORD said that he would dwell in the thick darkness [cloud]. I have surely built thee an house to dwell in, a settled place for thee to abide in for ever." (1 Kings 8:12–13; see also 2 Chronicles 6:1–2.)

Before dedicating the temple, Solomon addressed the people. He wanted them to understand that he had built the temple specifically to house the ark with its covenant contents. The rich and mighty king, creator of this lavish temple, knelt down in view of all Israel and spread his hands toward heaven. He humbly began the dedicatory prayer, "O LORD God of Israel, there is no God like thee in the heaven, nor in the earth; which keepest covenant . . . " (2 Chronicles 6:14; see also 1 Kings 8:23.) In the prayer he asked, "Will God in very deed dwell with men on the earth?" (2 Chronicles 6:18; see also 1 Kings 8:27.) He beseeched the Lord to hear the supplication and to open his eyes "upon this house day and night." (2 Chronicles 6:20; see also 1 Kings 8:29.)

When Solomon finished praying, the "fire came down from heaven, and consumed the burnt offering and the sacrifices; and the glory of the LORD filled the house. And the priests could not enter into the house of the LORD, because the glory of the LORD had filled the LORD's house. And when all the children of Israel saw how the fire came down, and the glory of the LORD upon the house, they bowed themselves with their faces to the ground upon the pavement, and worshipped, and praised the LORD." (2 Chronicles 7:1–3.)

Personal Acceptance

One night, after the dedication, the Lord appeared to Solomon. This probably occurred in the temple, for the Lord said, "I have heard thy prayer and thy supplication. . . . I have hallowed this house, which thou hast built, to put my name there for ever; and mine eyes and mine heart shall be there perpetually." (1 Kings 9:4; see also 2 Chronicles 7:12–16.)

Not only had all the people seen the Shechinah enter the temple, but Solomon personally saw the Lord. Jehovah, man, and covenant were finally united in a temple.

6

FROM GLORY TO DESOLATION

Five hundred years after the exodus, the Lord at last had a glorious temple in the land he had chosen for his people. Though generations of Israelites had become unworthy of the blessing, the Lord extended the opportunity to succeeding generations. At last, the Lord's patient, continuing effort had brought reward. With a house of the Lord in their midst, Israel was jubilant, at least for a while. As with us, their attitude toward and treatment of the temple indicated the status of their covenant with God.

A Serious Revolt

Although Solomon worthily built and dedicated the magnificent temple (1004 B.C.), he later fell from righteousness and took his people with him. Because of promises the Lord made to his father, the kingdom remained intact during his lifetime, but it was torn in two shortly after his death. When Solomon's son became king, the ten northern tribes revolted, forming a separate nation, the Kingdom of Israel. A mere twenty-nine years passed between the dedication of the temple and the revolt that left the northern kingdom without a temple. About 250 years later, as a direct result of losing the temple, the Kingdom of Israel fell to Assyria and the ten tribes were carried away and lost.

Elijah

In the meantime, the Lord sent the mighty prophet Elijah to the northern kingdom. Elijah challenged King Ahab and his prophets of Baal to a contest between gods. The true God would declare himself by igniting and consuming the appropriate sacrifice. All day long the priests of Baal appealed to their false and powerless god, Baal, to show his power, but to no avail. Elijah then carefully stacked the odds against his own God by drenching his altar and sacrifice with water that spilled over and filled a huge trench. When Elijah prayed, instantly the "fire of the LORD fell, and consumed the burnt sacrifice, and the wood, and the stones, and the dust, and licked up the water that was in the trench." (1 Kings 18:38; about 914 B.C.) The fire, thrown from a cloudless sky, proved the supreme power of that God who sent it. When the people saw it, they fell on their faces, for they recognized the fire of the true Lord—the same fire that consumed the first offering at both the tabernacle and the temple of Solomon.

Shortly after this, Elijah fled for his life. An angel fed him twice, and he, like Moses, "went in the strength of that meat forty days and forty nights unto Horeb the mount of God." (1 Kings 19:8; see also Exodus 34:18.) Also like Moses, he was told to "stand upon the mount before the LORD." (1 Kings 19:11.) As with Moses, a great wind came, then an earthquake, then a fire. The account continues, "but the LORD was not in the fire" (1 Kings 19:12.) Nevertheless, the record makes clear that, preceding the display of power, "the Lord passed by." (1 Kings 19:11.) Indeed, in the Pearl of Great Price, the Lord states, "I cause the wind and the fire to be my chariot." (Abraham 2:7.) If such was the case on this occasion, then Elijah saw the Shechinah. Elijah, again like Moses, talked personally with the Lord and received revelation from him.

Isaiah

Isaiah saw a vision of the Lord sitting on a throne in the temple. He saw the whole earth "full of his glory" and the house of God "filled with smoke." (Isaiah 6:3–4; about 758 B.C.) He also prophesied the Lord would ride "upon a swift cloud" into Egypt, and the idols there would be "moved at his presence," indicating the involvement of the Lord in the affairs of men outside Israel. (Isaiah 19:1.)

Prophesying of the Second Coming, Isaiah proclaimed, "the glory of the LORD shall be revealed, and all flesh shall see it together: for the mouth of the LORD hath spoken it." (Isaiah 40:5.)

Hezekiah

The same army that demolished the northern kingdom besieged the Kingdom of Judah. The king of Assyria sent a threatening, boastful letter mocking the God of Israel. King Hezekiah took this letter and "spread it before the LORD" in the temple. He pleaded with the "Lord God of Israel, which dwellest between the cherubims." (2 Kings 19:19; 712 B.C.) That night the angel of the Lord slew 185,000 Assyrian soldiers. Although the faithless northern kingdom was obliterated, the southern kingdom was saved by worthily petitioning the Lord in the temple.

Nebuchadnezzar

Over one hundred years later, King Nebuchadnezzar invaded Jerusalem and took treasures from the temple and led ten thousand captives, to Babylon. Although the people had polluted the temple, the

Lord had sent prophets "because he had compassion on his people, and on his dwelling place." Doom was now imminent for they "despised his words, and misused his prophets." (2 Chronicles 36:15–16.) Eleven years after the first invasions, Israel's puppet king, Zedekiah, rebelled. In response to the rebellion, Nebuchadnezzar returned and ransacked Jerusalem. The Chaldees "slew their young men with the sword in the house of their sanctuary. . . . And they burnt the house of God." (2 Chronicles 36:17–20; see also 2 Kings 25:9–17; 587 B.C.) The treasures from the house of the Lord, along with those captive people who escaped the sword, were carried away to Babylon.

It was poetic justice that the temple was destroyed by fire. The people had rejected their God, the very God who once sent his pillar of fire to guide and protect them. Because of their rejection, fire was now a power of destruction and cleansing. A fire of destruction and cleansing is prophesied for our day for the same reason.

The Departure of the Shechinah

During the vacillating and declining years of temple usage, no record was ever made of the glory of the Lord departing from the temple. As long as the ark of the covenant, or throne of God, remained, the glory remained with the earlier tabernacle (portable temple), even though the people generally apostatized. Though the outer areas of the temple were polluted, the ark of the covenant apparently stayed inside the Holy of Holies. The vision of Ezekiel provides scriptural indication that the Shechinah remained until the final destruction of the temple of Solomon.

Like the Shechinah, the ark of the covenant disappeared without Biblical record. Many Christian and Jews believe that, when the temple of Solomon was destroyed, the devout Jews hid the ark so that the invading king was not able to obtain it. Both the Talmud and the Apocrypha support this belief. Consequently at least three Americans have headed expeditions seeking the ark of the covenant. (See *Biblical Archaeology Review*, May/June 1983 and July/August 1983.)

The loss of the Shechinah is still lamented today through the Jewish fast day *Tisha b'Av* which recalls tragedies of the Jewish people. "The central mourning is over the destruction of the Temple. . . . This has both physical as well as spiritual dimensions. As Israel was divided from the land, so too was the Shekhinah—the Divine Presence." In addition, the fast day "represented the nature of the world's incompleteness and the great need for *tikkun*— repair (returning the Shekhinah to her place)." (Siegell, Strassfeld, and Strassfeld, *The First Jewish Catalog*, p. 148; note Hebrew spelling.) Returning the Shechinah to its place implies the return of a temple and specifically the ark of the covenant.

7

THE SHECHINAH IN VISION

The chosen people were in captivity seventy years. The Lord had not sent his people there to forget them but to chasten and prepare them. In fact, the Midrash (literature written during the first Christian millennium) maintains "that when Israel went into exile the Divine Presence joined them to comfort them in their homelessness." (Strassfeld and Strassfeld, *The Third Jewish Catalog*, p. 296.) This view is supported by the visions of Ezekiel and Daniel.

Daniel's Friends

During the last few years before Jerusalem was finally destroyed, thousands of Israelites were taken to Babylon. Daniel was one of these. When Daniel's three friends twice refused to worship Nebuchadnezzar's golden idol, the king furiously ordered them thrown into a raging furnace. Looking into the furnace, he asked incredulously, "Did not we cast three men bound into the midst of the fire? . . . I see four men loose, walking in the midst of the fire, and they have no hurt; and the form of the fourth is like the Son of God." (Daniel 3:24–25.) Nebuchadnezzar retrieved the three, who emerged unharmed without a hair or thread singed, without even the smell of fire on them. There are parallels to this in the Book of Mormon. (See 3 Nephi 28:21; 4 Nephi 1:32; Mormon 8:24.)

Ezekiel's First and Second Visions

Like Daniel, Ezekiel was carried off to Babylonia before Judah's final invasion. He was a priest by the river Chebar where many exiles lived. On one occasion he "looked, and behold, a whirlwind came out of the north, a great cloud, and a fire infolding itself, and a brightness was about it, and out of the midst thereof as the colour of amber, out of the midst of the fire." (Ezekiel 1:4; 593 B.C.)

Elijah was a great prophet who, like Moses and Elijah, witnessed the Shechinah. The Shechinah is the key to explain the incredible things he saw.

Ezekiel had difficulty conveying the vision he saw of a man upon a throne: "Upon the likeness of the throne was the likeness as the appearance of a man above upon it. And I saw as the colour of amber, as the appearance of fire round about within it, from the appearance of his loins even upward, and from the appearance of his loins even downward, I saw as it were the appearance of fire, and it had brightness round about. . . . This was the appearance of the likeness of the glory of the LORD." (Ezekiel 1:26–28.)

Ezekiel was so overwhelmed that he fell to his face. A voice said, "Stand upon thy feet. . . . I send thee to the children of Israel." (Ezekiel 2:1, 3.) Ezekiel was therefore called as a prophet to the children of Israel in captivity, much as Moses was.

On another occasion, the Lord told Ezekiel to go into the plain where the Lord would speak with him. Ezekiel recorded, "Behold, the glory of the LORD stood there, as the glory which I saw by the river of Chebar: and I fell on my face." (Ezekiel 3:23.) Again, Ezekiel saw the Shechinah. There was no temple in

Babylonia, not even a mountain, so the Lord appeared in the solitude of the plain.

Ezekiel's Third Vision

A year later as Ezekiel sat in his house, he saw a "likeness as the appearance of fire: from the appearance of his loins even downward, fire; and from his loins even upward, as the appearance of brightness, as the colour of amber. And he put forth the form of an hand, and . . . the spirit . . . brought me in the visions of God to Jerusalem, to the door of the inner gate [of the temple] that looketh toward the north. . . . And, behold, the glory of the God of Israel was there, according to the vision that I saw in the plain." (Ezekiel 8:2–4.) Once again, Ezekiel saw the Lord and his Shechinah in Babylonia, and then, transported by vision, in the temple at Jerusalem.

The vision revealed events that would occur in about five short years. Ezekiel saw in detail not only *why* but also *how* Judah would be destroyed. He saw the rampant idolatry practiced in the temple and throughout the land. The Lord who had decreed, "Thou shalt have no other gods before me" (Exodus 20:3) knew Israel's sin. This vision made it clear to Ezekiel why the enemy would invade.

In the vision the Lord called in a loud voice and "six men came from the way of the higher gate [of the temple], . . . every man a slaughter weapon in his hand; . . . and they went in, and stood beside the brasen altar." (Ezekiel 9:2.) These divinely charged officers reported for duty. This told how the destruction would begin.

"And the glory of the God of Israel was gone up from the cherub, whereupon he was, to the threshhold of the house." (Ezekiel 9:3.) Because the glory, or Shechinah, dwelt between the cherubim on the ark, moving from there to the doorway was unusual and significant. The Lord was stepping forward to direct the cleansing of his dwelling place, and he explained the battle plan. "Set a mark," he ordered, to distinguish the righteous. "Slay utterly" all others, and "begin at my sanctuary." (Ezekiel 9:4, 6.)

The Lord commanded a man clothed with linen, "Go in . . . and fill thine hand with coals of fire from between the cherubims, and scatter them over the city." (Ezekiel 10:2.) This told how the destruction would end in fire.

Ezekiel's vision was prophetic: first, slaughter by sword; second, devastation by fire. As Ezekiel saw, even so it became harsh reality. Slaughter began at the temple, and fire demolished Jerusalem.

A Tragic Loss

The foretold slaughter and destruction were terrible and complete, costing the Jews their lives and their nation. But the vision continued, revealing a loss even more devastating. Knowing what the Shechinah is and where it dwelt opens the vision to understanding.

Ezekiel saw that "the cherubims stood on the right side of the house [temple], when the man [in linen] went in; and the cloud filled the inner court. Then the glory of the LORD went up from the cherub, and stood over the threshold of the house; and the house was filled with the cloud, and the court was full of the brightness of the LORD's glory. . . . Then the glory of the LORD departed from off the threshold of the house, and stood over the cherubims. And the cherubims lifted up their wings, and mounted up from the earth in my sight . . . and every one stood at the door of the east gate of the LORD's house; and the glory of the God of Israel was over them above." (Ezekiel 10: 3–4 ,18–19.) The cherubim had moved, and the glory of the Lord with them, from inside the temple to the east gate. These details are significant.

After receiving final, personal instructions, Ezekiel saw "the cherubims lift up their wings; . . . and the glory of the God of Israel was over them above. And the glory of the LORD went up from the midst of the city, and stood upon the mountain which is on the east side of the city." (Ezekiel 11:22–23.)

This was the loss more tragic than the devastation of a nation. Here was a literal, as well as symbolic, loss of the presence of the Lord.

The glory of the Lord, or the Shechinah, left the temple to its destruction and moved to the mountain on the east. Since Ezekiel's vision was prophecy, it answered when and why the Shechinah left the temple of Solomon. Significantly, the cherubim, which guarded the Shechinah upon the mercy seat, went with it. Since the cherubim were attached to the seat, which was also the lid of the ark, it is probable that the ark of the covenant went to the east mountain. This prophecy, then, could give credibility to the Jewish tradition that the ark of the covenant was preserved when Assyria invaded.

Ezekiel's Vision of a New Temple

Even after the Shechinah left the temple, the Israelites were not deserted by the Lord. Still in exile, Ezekiel recorded a vision of hope and promise—a mountain in Jerusalem where a heavenly messenger showed and measured all the parts of a future temple. It is not incidental that the messenger walked Ezekiel through every room, measuring as he went. This temple will be built at a time when the Jews do not have a prophet to give them the building specifications. Knowing this, the Lord gave the blueprints to Ezekiel hundreds of years before needed, so they would be preserved in the scriptures. The detailed measuring covers three entire chapters. (Ezekiel 40–42.)

In our day, prophesy is becoming history. Major events preceding the building of the Jerusalem temple have already occurred. The nation of Israel has been restored (1948), and the city of Jerusalem has been taken by the Jews (1967). However, the Moslem mosque, Dome of the Rock, stands where the temple must be built. In 1961 the Jews began secretly gathering materials to build their temple. For example, in 1967, "500 railcar loads of stone . . . pre-cut to exact specifications" were sent to Israel for that purpose. (Skousen, *Fantastic Victory*, p. 282; quoting from *The Christian and Christianity Today*.) Obviously, the Jews knew what the exact specifications were. Ezekiel's vision, then, was not for his time but for ours.

In the vision, the messenger brought Ezekiel to the east gate of the future temple. "And, behold, the glory of the God of Israel came from the way of the east: And the earth shined with his glory. . . . And the glory of the LORD came into the house by the way of the gate whose prospect is toward the east." (Ezekiel 43:2, 4.)

It would be easy to pass over these short verses without realizing their import. Here is a glorious prophecy—the Shechinah will enter the future temple. This vision portends even greater significance when viewed as a companion to the previous one. The glory departed through the east gate in one vision and returned through the same gate in the other. As it departed, so will it return.

Ezekiel continued, "The spirit took me up, and brought me into the inner court; and, behold, the glory of the LORD filled the house. And . . . the man stood by me. And he said unto me, . . . [here is]

the place of my throne, . . . where I will dwell in the midst of the children of Israel for ever." (Ezekiel 43:5–7.)

Ezekiel was taken back to the east gate which was now shut. The Lord said, "This gate shall be shut, it shall not be opened, and no man shall enter in by it; because the LORD, the God of Israel, hath entered in by it, therefore it shall be shut." (Ezekiel 44:2.) (This is why our temples today face east, but the main entrance is elsewhere.)

"Then . . . I looked, and, behold, the glory of the LORD filled the house of the LORD: and I fell upon my face." (Ezekiel 44:4.) Ezekiel concluded the record of his vision, "and the name of the city from that day shall be, The LORD is there." (Ezekiel 48:35.)

Truly, the Lord will be there. He will enter his temple and use his throne as he told Ezekiel. In 1877, Orson Pratt, speaking of the future temple in Jerusalem, verified, "It will contain the throne of the Lord upon which he will, at times, personally sit." (Quoted by Ron Zeidner, *The Jews and the Second Coming,* Audio Tape. Covenant Communications, Inc., 1979.)

Ezekiel's prophecy verifies the Jewish tradition that the ark of the covenant will return. It indicates that the return will be literal. In addition, an explicit "written tradition" of its actual return is in the Apocrypha. This is separate from and in addition to both the oral Jewish tradition and written tradition in the Talmud. These "apocryphal writings were never included in the Hebrew Bible [Torah]." (McConkie, *Mormon Doctrine,* p. 41.) The Lord told Joseph Smith that the Apocrypha contains many things "that are true, and it is mostly translated correctly," and that "the Spirit manifesteth truth." (D&C 91:1, 4, 5.) Several verses relate to the ark of the covenant, its disappearance, and return.

Jeremiah was the prophet who personally witnessed the invasion and final destruction of Jerusalem.

> Prompted by a divine message, the prophet [Jeremiah] gave orders that the Tent of Meeting [Moses' tabernacle] and the ark should go with him. Then he went away to the mountain from the top of which Moses saw God's promised land.
> When he reached the mountain, Jeremiah found a cave-dwelling; he carried the tent, the ark, and the incense-altar into it, then blocked up the entrance.
> Some of his companions came to mark out the way, but were unable to find it. When Jeremiah learnt of this he reprimanded them. "The place shall remain unknown," he said, "until God finally gathers his people together and shows mercy to them.
> Then the Lord will bring these things to light again, and the glory of the Lord will appear with the cloud, as it was seen both in the time of Moses and when Solomon prayed that the shrine [temple] might be worthily consecrated." (Sandmel, New English Bible, 2 Maccabees 2:4–8.)

Various translations of this account begin by referring to a previous written record. A typical translation states, "We know from the records that Jeremiah the prophet" did these things. (The New Catholic Study Bible, 2 Maccabees 2:1.) In this version Jeremiah says to his friends, "No one must know about this place until God gathers his people together again and shows them mercy. At that time he will reveal where these things are hidden, and the dazzling light of his presence will be seen in the cloud, as it was in the time of Moses and on the occasion when Solomon prayed that the Temple might be dedicated in holy splendor." (2 Maccabees 2:7–8.)

Assuming the apocryphal record is accurate, Ezekiel's vision becomes explicit. Both accounts unite the return of the Shechinah and the return of the ark of the covenant, which is consistent with the ancient pattern. When this occurs, imagine the ecstatic jubilation of the Jews' celebration.

The ark of the covenant is not only the symbol of the Lord's kingship, but also the physical seat of his reign. The earth is his kingdom, and his throne will be in the palace-temple in Jerusalem. Our King's law, engraved in stone, was and may still be safeguarded inside the ark of the covenant. When the Lord comes to claim his kingdom, to rule and reign from his throne, it stands to reason his law will also return.

One thing is certain: Ezekiel saw an exciting vision showing the glory of the Lord, which dwelt above the ark, entering the temple from the east, where it had disappeared in the previous vision. It is a glorious promise to be fulfilled—the Shechinah will return. The Divine Presence will be in the temple and in the city. Perhaps the entry of the cloud into the tabernacle and into the Temple of Solomon are types foreshadowing the marvelous final entry which will fill the promised temple. At that time the Lord Jesus Christ will stay to dwell and rule and reign forever.

Daniel

While Ezekiel prophesied among the captives, Daniel lived in the royal courts. He saw a vision of Christ coming to the council in Adam-Ondi-Ahman before the Second Coming. He recorded, "One like the Son of man came with the clouds of heaven, and came to the Ancient of days [Adam], and they brought him [Adam] near before him [Christ]."

(Daniel 7:13.)

After a later vision, Daniel described the Lord's appearance. He was "clothed in linen, [and his] loins were girded with fine gold of Uphaz: His body also was like the beryl, and his face as the appearance of lightning, and his eyes as lamps of fire, and his arms and his feet like in colour to polished brass." (Daniel 10:5–6.) What Daniel described was the glory of the Lord.

Haggai's Prophecy

As a remnant of Jews returned to Jerusalem, the prophet Haggai instructed Zerubbabel, a direct descendent of King David and an ancestor of Jesus, to rebuild the temple. A month later, Haggai, speaking for the Lord asked, "Who is left among you that saw this house in her first glory? and how do ye see it now? is it not in your eyes in comparison of it as nothing? Yet now be strong . . . for I am with you, saith the LORD of hosts: According to the word that I covenanted with you when ye came out of Egypt, so my spirit remaineth among you: fear ye not." (Haggai 2:3–5.) Though the temple they built in poverty lacked the splendor of the former one, the Lord comforted them. What mattered was that he be with them.

Through Haggai, the Lord foretold the building of a third temple even grander than the first. "The desire of all nations [Jesus Christ] shall come: and I will fill this house with glory, saith the LORD of hosts. . . . The glory of this latter house shall be greater than of the former [Solomon's] saith the LORD of hosts." (Haggai 2:7, 9.) This temple, which will be built in Jerusalem, is the one where Ezekiel saw the glory return through the east gate. Knowing of the golden beauty of the first temple, it is hard to imagine how the future temple could be even greater. It will truly be spectacular, fit for its King, but its greatest splendor will be the glory of the Lord.

Temple of Zerubbabel

The temple of Zerubbabel was finished and dedicated with joy in 515 B.C. According to James E. Talmage, the temple of Zerubbabel lacked five features which were present in the temple of Solomon. Among them were the ark of the covenant, the sacred fire, and "the Shekinah, or glory of the Lord, manifested of old as the Divine Presence." Talmage commented further, "Notwithstanding these differences the Temple of Zerubbabel was recognized of God." (*The House of the Lord,* p. 42–43; see also the LDS Bible Dictionary, p. 783.) Although the temple of Zerubbabel lacked these gifts from the Lord, the Jews still look forward to their return.

Nehemiah

In Nehemiah's time, the people celebrated the Feast of the Tabernacles for the first time since Joshua's day. They recalled the Lord's guiding presence. "Moreover thou leddest them in the day by a cloudy pillar; and in the night by a pillar of fire, to give them light in the way wherein they should go. Thou camest down also upon mount Sinai, and speakest with them from heaven." (Nehemiah 9:12–13.)

Malachi

Malachi, final author in the Old Testament, testified that yet again the Lord "shall suddenly come to his temple, even the messenger of the covenant." (Malachi 3:1.) He knew that God, temple, and covenants were inseparable and essential for all generations.

Temple of Zerubbabel Restored

To curry the Jews favor, Herod began restoring
the temple of Zerubbabel in 17 B.C. The Jews, however, did not trust Herod. According to Talmage, they
"feared that were the ancient edifice demolished, . . .
the people would be left without a Temple. To allay
these fears the king proceeded to reconstruct and
restore the old edifice, part by part. . . . So little of
the ancient structure was allowed to stand, however,
that the Temple of Herod must be regarded as a new
creation." (*The House of the Lord*, p. 45–46.)

The Jews never did acknowledge Herod's rebuild-
ing as anything but a restoration of the temple of
Zerubbabel. The Wailing Wall yet standing today is
considered a remnant of the Second Temple. Perhaps
that segment, representing a time-span of nearly
twenty-five hundred years, will stand until the long-
awaited Third Temple, seen by Ezekiel and Haggai,
is built. Then the covenant people shall see for themselves what these prophets saw only in vision: the
return of the Shechinah.

8

THE SHECHINAH IN THE NEW TESTAMENT

Anciently, when the Lord dwelt among his people, they saw the glory surrounding him but did not see his person. When he lived among them in the flesh, they saw him but not his glory. A few, however, were privileged to see both.

Jesus' Mortal Ministry

Testifying that the Divine Son had been born into the world, the angel of the Lord appeared to the shepherds, and the "glory of the Lord shone round about them: and they were sore afraid." (Luke 2:9.) When Mary and Joseph took the infant to the temple, they met Simeon, who knowingly proclaimed the baby "the glory of thy people Israel." (Luke 2:32.)

By age twelve, Jesus was teaching in the temple, eager to be about "my Father's business." (Luke 2:49.) Those who asked him questions were amazed. Also amazed were the mourners who later watched Jesus raise a young man from the dead. Astonished, they chorused, "God hath visited his people." (Luke 7:16.) How literal this was, few understood.

Not only had the God of Israel visited his people, but, half-mortal, he dwelt among them. Often Jesus, the original lawgiver, taught in the temple which no longer contained his two tables of law. Built by despicable King Herod, the temple was without glory. Nevertheless Jesus called it "my Father's house" or "my house." As true owner of the house of the Lord, twice Jesus cleansed it. The Lord, his glory not apparent, walked there in person, teaching the people how to return to God, the same message he had taught in the temple for centuries.

One day near the end of his ministry, Jesus took Peter, James, and John, his brother, into a high mountain. There they saw him "transfigured before them: and his face did shine as the sun, and his raiment was white as the light." (Matthew 17:2.) Their master took on his divine glory. Then, "a bright cloud overshadowed them: and behold a voice out of the cloud, which said, This is my beloved Son, in whom I am well pleased; hear ye him." (Matthew 17:5.) According to this wording, the three would have been within the cloud; this is verified in a second, more detailed account.

As Jesus prayed, the "fashion of his countenance was altered, and his raiment was white and glistering. And, behold, there talked with him two men, which were Moses and Elias [Elijah]: Who appeared in glory. . . . But Peter and they that were with him were heavy with sleep: and when they were awake, they saw his glory, and the two men that stood with him." (Luke 9:29–32.) While Peter spoke, "There came a cloud, and overshadowed them: and they feared as they entered into the cloud. And there came a voice out of the cloud, saying, This is my Beloved Son: hear him." (Luke 9:34–35; see also Mark 9:2–7.)

To enter within the cloud must have been overwhelming. Although the heavenly messengers brought priesthood keys, the apostles did not record what happened within the cloud. Jesus warned them not to tell of their experience until after his resurrection. Without any doubt, they saw the glory of his godhood and witnessed his true identity.

Although most of the people refused to believe who Jesus was, Jesus knew he was the Son of God. In his last prayer with his apostles, he prayed, "And now, O Father, glorify thou me with thine own self with the glory which I had with thee before the world was." (John 17:5.)

Jesus boldly proclaimed his identity. At the trial of Jesus, the high priest ordered him, "I adjure thee by the living God, that thou tell us whether thou be the Christ, the Son of God." Jesus answered, "Thou hast said: nevertheless I say unto you, Hereafter shall ye see the Son of man sitting on the right hand of power, and coming in the clouds of heaven." (Matthew 26:63–64; see also Mark 14:61–62.) Thus Christ plainly taught how he would appear after his death, using the symbolism of the Shechinah, which the Jews understood, to represent his godhood. No wonder the high priest rent his clothes, denouncing Jesus as a blasphemer. The accused not only claimed to be the Son of God but also the God of the Old Testament—he who came in the clouds of heaven. Of course, that is exactly who he was.

Immediately after his resurrection, Jesus walked along the road to Emmaus with two travelers who grieved his death. In order to teach them, he asked, "Ought not Christ to have suffered these things, and to enter into his glory?" (Luke 24:26.) He knew the purpose of his suffering and the process by which his glory would come, and he wanted all men to understand also. It was foreknown that suffering would precede the glory.

For forty days following his resurrection, Jesus continued to teach his apostles. Then, on the mount of Olives, while they watched, "he was taken up; and a cloud received him out of their sight. And while they looked stedfastly toward heaven as he went up, behold, two men stood by them in white apparel; Which also said, Ye men of Galilee, why stand ye gazing up into heaven? this same Jesus, which is taken up from you into heaven, shall so come in like manner as ye have seen him go into heaven." (Acts 1:9–11.) All eleven faithful apostles witnessed his ascension in glory. This glory in itself testified of Jesus' majestic godhood.

"It is no wonder that the Son of Man, soon after his resurrection from the tomb, ascended to his Father," President Brigham Young observed, "for he had no place on earth to lay his head; his house still remaining in the possession of his enemies." (*Journal of Discourses* 8:30–31.)

John's Testimony

John began his gospel message with his eye-witness report of Christ's glory. "And the Word was made flesh, and dwelt among us, (and we beheld his glory, the glory as of the only begotten of the Father,) full of grace and truth." (John 1:14.) John had twice seen Christ in glory, at the transfiguration and at the ascension. In modern scripture the Lord affirms John's testimony, "John saw and bore record of the fulness of my glory." (D&C 93:6.) He quotes John as saying:

> And I, John, bear record that I beheld his glory, as the glory of the Only Begotten of the Father . . .
> And I, John, saw that he received not of the fulness at the first, . . . but continued from grace to grace, until he received a fulness; . . .
> And I, John, bear record that he received a fulness of the glory of the Father; . . .
> And he received all power, both in heaven and on earth, and the glory of the Father was with him, for he dwelt in him. (D&C 93:11–13, 16–17.)

Peter

Peter, like John, testified to the Saints of seeing the transfiguration. "For we have not followed cunningly devised fables, when we made known unto you the power and coming of our Lord Jesus Christ, but were eyewitness of his majesty. For he received from God the Father honour and glory, when there came such a voice to him from the excellent glory, This is my beloved Son, in whom I am well pleased. And this voice which came from heaven we heard, when we were with him in the holy mount." (2 Peter 1:16–18.)

Stephen

Stephen, one of seven assistants to the apostles, did "great works and miracles" which caught the attention of the Sanhedrin. Accused of changing the law of Moses, he defended himself by recounting Jewish history, including Moses seeing the presence of the Lord "in a flame of fire in a bush." (Acts 7:30; see also JST, Exodus 3:2.) Since Stephen's accusers were the guilty ones, they became angry. But Stephen, "being full of the Holy Ghost, looked up stedfastly into heaven, and saw the glory of God, and Jesus standing on the right hand of God." (Acts 7:55.) For this "crime," the council immediately stoned him.

Paul

Paul told his conversion story simply. "Suddenly," he said, "there shone from heaven a great light round about me." (Acts 22:6; see also Acts 9:3.) Paul's description sounds modest, yet he was so overpowered that he collapsed to the ground. Moses and Ezekiel had reacted to the Divine Presence in

the same way. Because Paul was well educated in
Jewish scriptures and traditions, most likely he
knew of the Shechinah. He probably recognized it,
for after hearing his name he answered, "Who art
thou, Lord?" (Acts 22:8.)

Moses had warned that no unrighteous man could
see God with the natural eye, and now this persecu-
tor of the Saints "could not see for the glory of that
light." (Acts 22:11.) Fellow travelers led the blind
man to Damascus where Ananias restored his sight.
Understanding what had happened, Ananias admon-
ished Paul, "The God of our fathers hath chosen thee,
that thou shouldest . . . see that Just One. . . . For
thou shalt be his witness . . . of what thou hast seen
and heard." (Acts 22:14–15.)

When Paul boldly reported his story to King
Agrippa, he added detail. "At midday, O king, I saw
in the way a light from heaven, above the brightness
of the sun, shining round about me." (Acts 26:13.)
Three times, Paul related his experience in the New
Testament. In each account, the Shechinah played a
prominent role in announcing the divine visitor. The
brilliant light, as well as the voice, testified, "I am
Jesus of Nazareth." (Acts 22:8; see also Acts 9:5,
Acts 26:15.)

Because of his powerful personal witness, Paul
preached forcefully of Christ. In Corinth, he taught
Gentile converts the Jewish heritage, or Christ's
dealings with ancient Israel. "Moreover, brethren, I
would not that ye should be ignorant how that all our
fathers were under the cloud, and all passed through
the sea." (1 Corinthians 10:1.) Paul taught the Jews
the nature of Christ. God has "spoken unto us by his
Son, . . . Who being the brightness of his glory, and the
express image of his person, . . . sat down on the right
hand of the Majesty on high." (Hebrews 1:2–4.) Paul
spoke convincingly from experience.

John's Revelation

John had already borne testimony of seeing our Lord in immortal glory. Years later, on the isle of Patmos, he heard the Lord's great voice behind him. Turning, John saw "one like unto the Son of man, clothed with a garment down to the foot, and girt about the paps with a golden girdle. His head and his hairs were white like wool, as white as snow; and his eyes were as a flame of fire; And his feet like unto fine brass, as if they burned in a furnace; . . . and his countenance was as the sun shineth in his strength." (Revelation 1:12–16; see also Revelation 2:18.) Without question this was the resurrected Christ in his glory for he announced himself, "I am he that liveth, and was dead; and, behold, I am alive for evermore." (Revelation 1:18.) John, who personally saw Jesus in glory at the transfiguration and the ascension, saw him again in immortal glory.

Prophesy Fulfilled

Jesus himself, and his apostles after him, repeatedly testified from personal knowledge that he was the Son of God. Nevertheless, just as the children of Israel had forsaken their God in times past, the Jews denied him in person. Their ancestors had lost the splendid temple of Solomon because they had rejected Jehovah. Jesus had prophesied that the Jews would lose the temple of Herod for the same reason.

The disciples had asked Jesus, "Show us concerning the buildings of the temple, as thou hast said—They shall be thrown down, and left unto you desolate." He answered graphically, "There shall not be left here, upon this temple, one stone upon another that shall not be thrown down." (Joseph Smith—Matthew 1:2–3.)

Constantly under construction during Jesus' lifetime, the temple of Herod was finally completed after seventy-nine years. Only eight years later, exactly as Christ had told his disciples, it was demolished in the Roman siege in 70 A.D. Neither the Lord nor his house was left upon the earth, and nearly two thousand years marched by before either returned.

9

THE SHECHINAH IN ANCIENT AMERICA

We need to remember that the Book of Mormon people were not just early Indians but were actually of the favored tribe of Joseph. Their ancestors saw Sinai smoking and saw the cloud filling the temple of Solomon on dedication day. They left the promised land behind for a new inheritance just before the Jewish nation, city, and temple were obliterated.

The Nephites built at least three temples. After the Lord's resurrection, he appeared on the temple grounds in Bountiful. With this exception, manifestations of the presence of the Lord in ancient America appear in other settings.

Brother of Jared

The earliest Book of Mormon incidence of the Shechinah occurred long before Moses went to the holy mount, in fact, long before Abraham fathered the covenant people. At the time of the tower of Babel, not long after Noah's time, a family group left the area, led by the Lord. In a valley, "the Lord came down and talked with the brother of Jared; and he was in a cloud, and the brother of Jared saw him not. . . . The Lord did go before them, and did talk with them as he stood in a cloud, and gave directions whither they should travel." (Ether 2:4–5.) The Lord intended to take them to a choice land where they must serve him or be swept off.

In the meantime, the group moved to the seashore, where they camped in tents for four years without praying for direction. Finally "the Lord came again unto the brother of Jared, and stood in a cloud and talked with him" for three hours. (Ether 2:14.) The first message was chastisement; the second, instruction for shipbuilding. In parallel to the story of Moses, a Shechinah appearance of the Lord provided direction to a promised land.

Lehi

Lehi saw a vision which caused him to leave Jerusalem. This vision, probably recorded in the lost book of Lehi, is alluded to in Nephi's record. Nephi mentioned that as Lehi was praying, "there came a pillar of fire and dwelt upon a rock before him; and he saw and heard much; and because of the things which he saw and heard he did quake and tremble exceedingly." (1 Nephi 1:6.) The "pillar of fire" was the Shechinah. This clue reveals the significance of Lehi's vision—the Lord came and talked to him.

No wonder that after this experience, Lehi was so overwhelmed that he went home and collapsed on his bed. Then in vision he saw the heavens open and "One descending out of the midst of heaven, and he beheld that his luster was above that of the sun at noon-day." (1 Nephi 1:9.) Apparently, the second experience reaffirmed the first. As with Moses and the brother of Jared, a brilliant appearance of the Lord provided direction to a promised land.

Before his death, Lehi spoke to his rebellious sons, reminding them, "I have beheld his glory." (2 Nephi 1:15.)

Nephi

When convincing his brothers of the power and goodness of the Lord, Nephi cited many examples from early Israel. One was the Lord "going before them, leading them by day and giving light unto them by night." (1 Nephi 17:30.) Knowledge of the Shechinah obviously went with the Nephites to the new world.

Jacob

In Lehi's farewell to his son Jacob, he mentioned, "Thou hast beheld in thy youth his glory." (2 Nephi 2:4.) We do not have Jacob's record of this event; however, Nephi confirmed it when he said, "My brother, Jacob, also has seen him [the Redeemer] as I have seen him." (2 Nephi 11:3.) In other words, both men saw the Lord in his glory.

Alma

Alma, at about 82 B.C., eagerly prepared his people for the Lord's coming. He explained, "Not many days hence the Son of God shall come in his glory; and his glory shall be the glory of the Only Begotten of the Father." (Alma 9:26.) Awaiting this joyous time, Alma taught that angels were "preparing the hearts of the children of men to receive his word at the time of his coming in his glory." (Alma 13:24.) Alma was referring to the coming of the resurrected Savior to the Nephite people.

Nephi and Lehi

One of the most unique Shechinah appearances occurred when two missionary brothers, Nephi and Lehi were imprisoned and surrounded by the Lamanites. Then "Nephi and Lehi were encircled about as if by fire, even insomuch that they [the Lamanites] durst not lay their hands upon them for fear lest they should be burned. Nevertheless, Nephi and Lehi were not burned; and they were as standing in the midst of fire and were not burned. And when they saw that they were encircled about with a pillar of fire, and that it burned them not, their hearts did take courage. . . . [The Lamanites] were overshadowed with a cloud of darkness." (Helaman 5:23–24, 28.) The Shechinah appeared to the Lamanites as it had appeared to the ancient Egyptians, as a cloud of darkness. This cloud caused fear, and the voice coming from it commanded them, "Repent!" This voice was the final clue to recognizing the Shechinah, for someone was within the pillar of fire and the cloud.

A Nephite dissenter in the group "saw through the cloud of darkness the faces of Nephi and Lehi; and behold, they did shine exceedingly, even as the faces of angels." (Helaman 5:36.)

The crowd of three hundred turned to Aminadab, the Nephite, asking what they could do to remove the cloud. He answered that they should repent, and pray, and have faith in Christ. Then "they all did begin to cry unto the voice of him who had shaken the earth; yea, they did cry even until the cloud of darkness was dispersed. And it came to pass that when they cast their eyes about, and saw that the cloud of darkness was dispersed from overshadowing them, behold, they saw that they were encircled about, yea every soul, by a pillar of fire. And Nephi and Lehi were in the midst of them; yea, they were encircled about; yea, they were as if in the midst of a flaming fire, yet it did harm them not." (Helaman 5:41–44.)

This was a marvelous experience with the Shechinah. As soon as the Lamanites repented and their spiritual level increased, instead of a cloud of darkness, they saw the pillar of fire. Apparently the manifestation of the Shechinah did not change, but rather their ability to see. Indeed, they went from outside to within its influence.

Appearance of Christ

Surprisingly, the description of Christ appearing to the Nephites barely mentions his glory. The first report, inserted by Mormon, is matter-of-fact. "Soon after the ascension of Christ into heaven [from Jerusalem] he did truly manifest himself unto them." (3 Nephi 10:18.)

The survivors, gathered around the temple in Bountiful, three times heard a voice. "As they understood they cast their eyes up again towards heaven; and behold, they saw a Man descending out of heaven; and he was clothed in a white robe; and he came down and stood in the midst of them." (3 Nephi 11:8.) Incredibly, they did not even know who he was. They were frightened and did not know "what it meant, for they thought it was an angel that had appeared unto them." (3 Nephi 11:8.) The divine visitor had to plainly introduce himself, "Behold, I am Jesus Christ." (3 Nephi 11:10.) Then the people fell to the earth and worshiped, remembering the prophesies that he would show himself to them.

Jesus lovingly ministered, teaching and healing the people. They were overcome with joy by his prayer for them. Jesus, too, was full of joy, and wept. After tenderly blessing the little children one by one, he again wept with joy. He told the multitude to look toward heaven, and "they saw the heavens open, and they saw angels descending out of heaven as it were in the midst of fire; and they came down and encircled those little ones about, and they were encircled about with fire; and the angels did minister unto them." (3 Nephi 17:24.)

The marvelous day came to a close with Jesus bestowing his twelve chosen disciples with the power to give the Holy Ghost. "And it came to pass that when Jesus had touched them all [the twelve], there came a cloud and overshadowed the multitude that they could not see Jesus. And while they were overshadowed he departed from them, and ascended into heaven. And the disciples saw and did bear record that he ascended again into heaven." (3 Nephi 18:38–39.) Thus, although there was no mention of cloud or fire on his arrival, Jesus left in a cloud.

The next day the people prayed, preached, and baptized, preparing for his return. After all were baptized, "the Holy Ghost did fall upon them, and they were filled with the Holy Ghost and with fire. And behold, they were encircled about as if it were by fire; and it came down from heaven, and the multitude did witness it." (3 Nephi 19:13–14.) Angels came out of heaven and ministered. Lastly, the record states simply, "Jesus came and stood in the midst." (3 Nephi 19:15.)

Asking the multitude to kneel in prayer, Jesus likewise knelt a little ways from them. He finished to find his disciples still praying. He blessed them and "the light of his countenance did shine upon them, and behold they were as white as the countenance and also the garments of Jesus; and behold the whiteness thereof did exceed all the whiteness, yea, even there could be nothing upon earth so white as the whiteness thereof." (3 Nephi 19:25.) Jesus then turned and prayed again. When he finished the second time, the disciples still prayed without ceasing, and "he did smile upon them again; and behold they were white, even as Jesus." (3 Nephi 19:30.) Thus, Jesus did shine with white radiance in his personal appearance to the Nephites.

Jesus then taught the congregation "all things, even from the beginning until the time that he

should come in his glory." (3 Nephi 26:3.) As glorious
as his coming was among the Nephites, it merely
foreshadowed the coming we eagerly await.

Of his leaving the second day, the account simply
states that Christ "ascended into heaven." (3 Nephi
26:15.) For the Nephites, the Shechinah was not the
focus; the cloud of fiery glory that enfolded him was
merely a sign. The Israelites, hearing the Lord's
voice from this cloud, had trembled. The Jews, seeing
the Lord, had rejected and crucified him. But the
Nephites, both hearing and seeing the Lord, rejoiced
and basked in his majestic presence.

10

THE SHECHINAH IN MODERN AMERICA

Joseph Smith

A young teenage boy, who had been taught that the three members of the Godhead were somehow one, inseparable, and intangible, received a glorious answer to prayer in 1820. In his own account of that experience, Joseph Smith wrote that immediately after kneeling, a power of dark destruction overcame him, but "just at this moment of great alarm, I saw a pillar of light exactly over my head, above the brightness of the sun, which descended gradually until it fell upon me. . . . When the light rested upon me I saw two Personages, whose brightness and glory defy all description, standing above me in the air. One of them spake unto me, calling me by name and said, pointing to the other—*This is My Beloved Son. Hear Him!*" (Joseph Smith—History 1:16–17.)

Joseph, like prophets before him, was overwhelmed by his first vision. "When I came to myself again, I found myself lying on my back, looking up into heaven. When the light had departed, I had no strength." (Joseph Smith—History 1:20.)

To his amazement, this young man unexpectedly saw the Son of God. The Lord came not in fire and smoke but in his brilliant glory. This was the first modern-day appearance of the Shechinah.

Joseph Smith established the Lord's church on April 6, 1830. Not quite two years later, he and Sidney Rigdon unitedly recorded that "by the power of the Spirit our eyes were opened." (D&C 76:12.) They testified of "Jesus Christ, who is the Son, whom we saw and with whom we conversed in the heavenly vision. . . . And the glory of the Lord shone round about. And we beheld the glory of the Son, on the right hand of the Father." Their testimony emphasized: "He lives! For we saw him." (D&C 76:14, 19–20, 23.)

Kirtland Temple

On May 6, 1833, when the Church was three years old, Joseph Smith received instruction to build a house for the Lord. The revelation gave Joseph a promise and a warning: "My glory shall be there, and my presence shall be there. But if there shall come into it any unclean thing, my glory shall not be there; and my presence shall not come into it." (D&C 94:8–9.)

The first modern-day temple was completed in Kirtland, Ohio. On Wednesday, March 27, 1836, it was dedicated by Joseph Smith in a prayer given to him by revelation.

> Thanks be to thy name, O Lord God of Israel, who keepest covenant.
> . . . We ask thee, O Lord, to accept of this house . . . which thou didst command us to build.
> For thou knowest that we have done this work through great tribulation . . . that the Son of Man might have a place to manifest himself to his people.
> We ask thee to assist us, . . . that we may be found worthy, in thy sight, to secure a fulfilment of the promises which thou hast made unto us, thy people, in the revelations given unto us;
> That thy glory may rest down upon thy people, and upon this thy house . . . and that thy holy presence may be continually in this house.

> . . . And that this house may be . . . a house of
> glory and of God, even thy house. (D&C 109:1,
> 4–5, 10–12, 16.)

The dedicatory prayer included this request: "Let it
be fulfilled upon [thy ministers], as upon those on the
day of Pentecost; let the gift of tongues be poured out
upon thy people, even cloven tongues as of fire. . . .
And let thy house be filled, as with a rushing mighty
wind, with thy glory." (D&C 109:36–37.) Immediate
fulfillment came.

The official *History of the Church* records the following:

> Brother George A. Smith arose and began to
> prophesy, when a noise was heard like the sound of
> a rushing mighty wind, which filled the Temple,
> and all the congregation simultaneously arose,
> being moved upon by the invisible power; many
> began to speak in tongues and prophesy; others
> saw glorious visions; and I beheld the Temple was
> filled with angels, which fact I declared to the con-
> gregation. The people of the neighborhood came
> running together (hearing an unusual sound
> within, and seeing a bright light like a pillar of fire
> resting upon the Temple), and were astonished at
> what was taking place. This continued until the
> meeting closed at eleven p.m. (2:428.)

Not only did the people of Kirtland, who were
non-Mormons, see the pillar of fire, but they thought
the new building was burning. The event was
reported as such in the newspaper. But this was no
ordinary fire. As with the tabernacle in the wilderness and the temple of Solomon, the Shechinah was
evident at the dedication of the Kirtland temple. The
Lord had literally fulfilled his promise, given with
the command to build the temple, "My glory shall be
there, and my presence shall be there." (D&C 94:8;
see also D&C 97:15–16.)

As the climax of the dedicatory service, the choir and congregation sang "The Spirit of God" with great emotion and spiritual power. The words fit the occasion:

> The Spirit of God like a fire is burning!
> The latter-day glory begins to come forth;
> The visions and blessings of old are returning,
> And angels are coming to visit the earth.
>
> [Chorus:] We'll sing and we'll shout with the
>   armies of heaven,
> Hosanna, hosanna to God and the Lamb!
> Let glory to them in the highest be given,
> Henceforth and forever, Amen and amen!
> (*Hymns*, p. 2.)

This hymn included words of the Hosanna shout used in all temple dedications.

Eliza R. Snow reported, "No mortal language can describe the heavenly manifestations of that memorable day. Angels appeared to some, while a sense of divine presence was realized by all. . . . Not only did the Almighty manifest his acceptance of that house, at its dedication, but . . . on subsequent occasions . . . a pillar of light was several times seen resting down upon the roof." (Jenson, *Historical Record,* Vol. 5, p. 79.)

A week later, on April 3, Joseph Smith and Oliver Cowdery witnessed another appearance in the temple, just as they were concluding a fervent prayer.

> We saw the Lord standing upon the breastwork of the pulpit, before us; and under his feet was a paved work of pure gold, in color like amber.
>
> His eyes were as a flame of fire; the hair of his head was white like the pure snow; his countenance shone above the brightness of the sun; and his voice was as the sound of the rushing of great waters, even the voice of Jehovah, saying:

. . . For behold, I have accepted this house, and my name shall be here; and I will manifest myself to my people in mercy in this house.

Yea, I will appear unto my servants, and speak unto them with mine own voice, if my people will keep my commandments, and do not pollute this holy house. (D&C 110:2–3, 7–8.)

Nauvoo Temple

In January of 1841, the Lord asked for a temple in Nauvoo. "Come ye, with all your gold, and your silver, and your precious stones, . . . and with all your precious things of the earth; and build a house to my name for the Most High to dwell therein." (D&C 124:26–27.)

Though the Nauvoo temple was never fully completed, some of the rooms were privately dedicated and used. In addition, on Sunday, February 8, 1846, Brigham Young "met with the Council of the Twelve. . . . We knelt around the altar, and dedicated the building to the Most High. . . . we would leave it in his hands to do as he pleased." (*History of the Church* 7:580.)

The next day, when the roof accidentally caught fire, Brigham Young commented, "If it is the will of the Lord that the Temple be burned, instead of being defiled by the Gentiles, Amen to it." (*History of the Church* 7:581.) However, the building stood, and he lamented, "I hoped to see it burned before I left but I did not." (*Journal of Discourses* 8:203.)

While Brigham Young was on the trail west, Orson Hyde returned to the depopulated city to dedicate the temple on three consecutive days (May 1–3). Endowments were never given afterward. As President Young feared, soldiers occupied and desecrated the building before it was destroyed by an arsonist's torch in October, 1848.

Logan Temple

At an address at the dedication of the Logan Temple on May 18, 1884, President John Taylor said, "It has been . . . expressed by some, that we ought to look for some peculiar manifestations. The question is, What do we want to see? Some peculiar power, some remarkable manifestations? All these things are very proper in their place; all these things we have a right to look for; but we must only look for such manifestations as are requisite for our circumstances, and as God shall see fit to impart them. Certain manifestations have already occurred." (*Journal of Discourses* 25:177.) In other words, do not expect to see the Shechinah at the dedication of this temple.

However, after the dedication, President Taylor recorded an experience like Solomon's and Joseph Smith's. The Savior accepted the newly dedicated temple: "As thou hast asked me concerning this Temple, thus saith the Lord: I accept this House which thou hast built . . . And inasmuch as it shall be preserved pure and not be defiled, my presence shall be there even the power of my Spirit: The Gift of the Holy Ghost, which shall in this House hereafter be more fully understood." (Reay, *Selected Manifestations,* p. 116; quoting from John Taylor Papers in the Church Historian's Office.)

Some years later, a heavenly manifestation occurred at the Logan Temple. One night as the temple president was on his way home, he "turned to tell the temple good-bye as was his custom, and his heart about jumped out of his body. He could see the temple was on fire, but as he looked at it for a few minutes he was satisfied that there were no red flames licking upwards. The whole temple was filled with light, and the outside of the building shone with a pale pink glow. All the people in the neighborhood gathered to watch the phenomena. . . . Everyone marveled at the sight, for there were no electric lights or other means of lighting the building. . . . The same thing happened the following night." (Olsen, *Logan Temple: The First 100 Years*, p. 175.)

When this heavenly manifestation was reported to President Wilford Woodruff, he asked what special work had been done in the temple. The Hale family, in a week-long reunion, had done baptisms, endowments, and sealings for four thousand family members. President Woodruff said the family had been permitted to rejoice in their deliverance in the Logan Temple. The "fire" in and on the building suggests that they may have had a divine escort.

Manti Temple

A personal journal of an early Saint describes the dedication of the Manti Temple in 1888. "The spirit and power of God was there, the glory of God was there, and it shone around some of the speakers." (Heinerman, *Temple Manifestations*, p. 95.)

Salt Lake Temple

Dedication services for the Salt Lake Temple ran from April 6 through April 24, 1893. An official Church publication, the *Contributor,* printed a commemorative issue for the dedication. It stated: "There was an influence present which it is not in the power of mortal man to describe. It had to be felt in order to be appreciated, and it seems without exception that everyone who attended did partake of the influence which pervaded." ("The Salt Lake Temple," *Contributor,* April, 1893, p. 304.)

Wilford Woodruff, on the second day of the Salt Lake Temple dedication, testified: "I feel at liberty to reveal to this assembly this morning what has been revealed to me since we were here yesterday morning. If the veil could be taken from our eyes . . . we could see into the spirit world. . . . In the midst of these spirits we would see the Son of God, the Savior, who presides and guides and controls the preparing of the kingdom of God on the earth and in heaven. . . . The dedication is acceptable in the eyes of the Lord." (Bennett, *Saviors on Mount Zion,* p. 142–43; quoting from a stenographic report of the services.) President Woodruff's revelation reflects the previous pattern of the Lord personally accepting a new temple. An official report of the dedication verifies this. "[The Saints'] toils and sacrifices for forty years were crowned in glorious triumph by the revelation from God that He accepted of the Temple as a habitation holy to His name." ("The Salt Lake Temple," *Contributor,* April, 1893, p. 302.)

A severely violent wind raged for two hours on the morning of the dedication causing enormous damage—"as if 'the prince of the power of the air' was giving vent to his fiercest wrath." ("The Salt Lake Temple," *Contributor,* April, 1893, p. 292.) The reward for building the temple, however, was "partially found in the prophecy of President Woodruff, that from this time Satan would no more have the power which he has heretofore held against the people of God, but they should become stronger as time should pass until they had reached that perfection for which we are so earnestly striving." ("The Salt Lake Temple," *Contributor,* April, 1893, p. 304.) Today we enjoy continuing protection through our temples, according to that prophecy, as we continue to strive for that perfection.

Since its dedication, the Salt Lake Temple has been the home of countless private spiritual experiences. President Lorenzo Snow shared with his granddaughter, Allie Young Pond, his experience of seeing the Savior. She wrote,

> Grandpa came a step nearer and held out his left hand and said: "He stood right here [in the large corridor leading into the Celestial Room], about three feet above the floor. It looked as though He stood on a plate of solid gold."
>
> Grandpa told me what a glorious personage the Savior is and described His hands, feet, and countenance and beautiful white robes, all of which were of such glory of whiteness and brightness that he could hardly gaze upon him. Then he came another step nearer and put his right hand on my head and said: "Now, granddaughter, I want you to remember that this is the testimony of your grandfather, that he told you with his own lips that he actually saw the Savior, here in the Temple, and talked with Him face to face." (Lundwall, *Temples of the Most High*, p. 145.)

In 1917, Melvin J. Ballard, not yet an apostle, dreamed he was in the Salt Lake Temple. "I was informed that I should have the privilege of [meeting] . . . a glorious Personage, and as I entered the door, I saw, seated on a raised platform, the most glorious Being my eyes have ever beheld. . . . He took me into his arms and kissed me, pressed me to his bosom, and blessed me, until the marrow of my bones seemed to melt! When he had finished, I fell at his feet, and as I bathed them with my tears and kisses, I saw the prints of the nails in the feet of the Redeemer." (Hinckley, *Sermons and Missionary Services of Melvin J. Ballard*, p. 156.) Elder Ballard added, "Oh! if I could live worthy . . . so that in the end when I have finished I could go into His presence and receive the feeling that I then had in His presence. I would give everything that I am and ever hope to be!" (Bookcraft, *Melvin J. Ballard—Crusader for Righteousness,* p. 66.) Oh! that we could somehow sear upon our hearts that same burning desire.

Many years later, a Salt Lake Temple president recalled an experience in the solemn assembly room of that temple. About three hundred departing missionaries met in a question-answer session with Harold B. Lee, President of the Church. One young elder asked, "President Lee, does the Savior ever visit the Salt Lake Temple?" After a moment's reflection, the Lord's spokesman answered, "How do you know he is not here now? This is his house." (Edmunds, *Through Temple Doors,* p. 22.)

Yes, the temple is his house. As he has told us, if we keep the temples holy, he will sanctify them by his presence.

Arizona Temple

Not long ago, L. Harold Wright, former Arizona Temple president, recalled escorting Mark E. Peterson (then an apostle, now deceased) to the Arizona temple during off-hours, at his request. Leaving the apostle alone, President Wright returned after the appointed half-hour. Elder Peterson, indicating the landing at the top of the stairs outside the celestial room, said he had seen the Savior there just ten minutes before. Though we normally do not see the Lord or his Shechinah, we who enter the temple walk where Jesus walks.

11

THE SHECHINAH AND THE HOLY GHOST

A major bridge from studying the glory of Christ to progressing toward our own glory is to understand the nature of this mysterious fire, the Shechinah. A discourse by Orson Pratt tells us what it is. He declared that the Holy Ghost is the "same fire that rested upon the tabernacle and camp of Israel, for forty years in the wilderness. . . . It was this same fire that filled the temple of Solomon at the time of its dedication. It is this same fire that surrounds the Holy One of Israel." (Lundwall, *Discourses on the Holy Ghost*, p. 37.) The word *Shechinah* could accurately be substituted for the word *fire*.

The Book of Mormon shows that the "light of the glory of God" and the light of the Holy Ghost are synonymous. Ammon spoke of "the light which did light up his [Lamanite king's] mind, which was the light of the glory of God." (Alma 19:6.) We recognize that the Holy Ghost was at work. The light was of the Holy Ghost and also of the glory of God. By logical reasoning, therefore, the light of the Holy Ghost and the light of the glory of God are the same thing.

The Shechinah is a manifestation of the Lord Jesus Christ. The Holy Ghost, as a member of the Godhood, has a twofold mission: 1) to testify of Christ and 2) to purify us. One way he testifies of Christ, who is already pure, is by a fire surrounding Christ's personage. Thus, the Shechinah, or glory of the Lord, comes through the Holy Ghost. Visible shining comes from being filled with the Holy Ghost.

The Holy Ghost purifies us through the baptism of fire. Jesus set the example for us to follow in order to become like him, which includes receiving eternal glory. On earth, he was baptized by water. At his transfiguration, receiving his glory, he was also baptized by the spirit. Elder Pratt emphasized the importance of our receiving both baptisms. "The promise is, that Jesus who was himself baptized with the Holy Ghost, should confer this same glorious baptism upon all his children. The two baptisms . . . are the same that all men must receive, in order to become the sons of God." (Lundwall, *Discourses on the Holy Ghost*, p. 35.)

Baptism of Fire

John the Baptist baptized with water and taught that One mightier than himself (that is, Christ) "shall baptize you with the Holy Ghost and with fire . . . he will burn up the chaff with unquenchable fire." (Matthew 3:11–12; see also Luke 3:16.) The "chaff" is sin. The baptism of fire, Orson Pratt said, refers to "the purifying qualities of the Holy Ghost, which like fire, consumes or destroys the unholy affections" of those who receive it. (Lundwall, *Discourses on the Holy Ghost*, p. 35.)

Bruce R. McConkie explained it this way: "By the power of the Holy Ghost—who is the Sanctifier— dross, iniquity, carnality, sensuality, and every evil thing is burned out of the repentant soul as if by fire. . . . The baptism of fire is not something in addition to the receipt of the Holy Ghost; rather, it is the actual enjoyment of the gift which is offered by the laying on of hands at the time of baptism." (McConkie, *Mormon Doctrine*, p. 73.)

A Fire That Consumes Not

While the Holy Ghost burns like fire, destroying impurities, it does not consume the righteous. When Nephi and Lehi were in a Lamanite prison, a mob of three hundred came to kill them. After a divine manifestation, the Lamanites repented, and "they were encircled about, yea every soul, by a pillar of fire. . . . [Nephi and Lehi] were as if in the midst of a flaming fire, yet it did harm them not, neither did it take hold upon the walls of the prison; and they were . . . full of glory. And behold, the Holy Spirit of God did come down from heaven, and did enter into their hearts, and they were filled as if with fire." (Helaman 5:43–45.) Being "full of glory" is synonymous with being "filled" with the "fire" of the Holy Ghost.

Christ referred to this incident when he taught the Nephites. "And whoso cometh unto me with a broken heart and a contrite spirit, him will I baptize with fire and the Holy Ghost, even as the Lamanites, because of their faith in me at the time of their conversion, were baptized with fire and with the Holy Ghost, and they knew it not." (3 Nephi 9:20.) The "fire" of the Holy Ghost sanctified them.

The next day, Jesus' listeners had the same experience. Nephi baptized the people, and when they "had come up out of the water, the Holy Ghost did fall upon them, and they were filled with the Holy Ghost and with fire. And behold, they were encircled about as if it were by fire; and it came down from heaven, and the multitude did witness it, and did bear record." (3 Nephi 19:13–14.)

Filled with the Holy Ghost

Nephi and Lehi, and the Nephites with Jesus, were all filled with the Holy Ghost. On the day of Pentecost the Saints "were all filled with the Holy Ghost." (Acts 2:4.) The term *filled* has interesting ramifications. Stephen, when defending himself before the Sanhedrin, was "full" of the Holy Ghost and shone. When Nephi was convincing his brothers to help build the ship, he told them, "I am full of the Spirit of God." He commanded them not to harm him for, he said, "I am filled with the power of God, even unto the consuming of my flesh; and whoso shall lay his hands upon me shall wither even as a dried reed." They dared not touch him, "so powerful was the Spirit of God." (1 Nephi 17:47, 48, 52.)

A modern day description of this phenomenon occurred in a meeting of the Quorum of Seventy held February 6, 1836 when "many arose and spoke, testifying that they were filled with the Holy Ghost, which was like fire in their bones." (Heinerman, *Temple Manifestations,* p. 27; quoting from *Documentary History of the Church* 2:392.)

Although Orson Pratt did not use the term *filled,* he showed the cause and effect relationship that the Holy Ghost had on Moses: "Moses was baptized with the Holy Ghost and with fire, so that when he came down from mount Sinai, after being with the Lord many days, his face shone with that brilliancy that the children of Israel could not endure the brightness and intensity of the light, but fled and stood afar off. Moses was obliged to veil his face to hide the glory of his countenance from Israel. (Lundwall, *Discourses on the Holy Ghost,* p. 37.) This clearly shows that the Holy Ghost causes shining and glory in a physical body.

Dwelling with God

Through the baptism of fire, Moses was prepared to walk and talk, even dwell, with the Lord. The preparation process is the same today. B. H. Roberts, a former Church historian, wrote that repentance, baptism by water, and baptism of the Spirit are the means whereby men's bodies are "made fit dwelling places for the Holy Ghost—the living temples of God." (Lundwall, *Discourses on the Holy Ghost,* p. 63.)

We look forward to the day when we can dwell with God. But through the Holy Ghost, this is possible now. "The man who is confirmed receives, in addition to this Spirit of Christ, the companionship of the third member of the Godhead. Therefore, he is back again in the Presence of God, through the gift of the Holy Ghost." (Smith, *Doctrines of Salvation,* 1:41.)

The fire of the Holy Ghost, then, sanctifies us and prepares us for further glory. The glory of God, or the Shechinah, although magnified beyond our comprehension, is the same physical matter as we receive through the baptism of fire. Christ burns with a brilliant blaze; we flicker with a tiny flame. Orson Pratt clarified that the brilliant fire and glory of Christ come through the Holy Ghost. Our little lights come from the same source.

Any of us who have received the gift of the Holy Ghost are entitled to his companionship. The more purified we become, the more filled we will be by his spirit. In a real way, we can grow in the amount of light we have from the Holy Ghost that surrounds us. Eventually we can shine with a glory of our own.

12

THE COVENANT
OFFER RESTORED

Once we have been baptized by water and by fire, we are on the path leading to the gate of heaven. The gate of heaven is the temple. (See Genesis 28:17.) Nephi emphasized, "The keeper of the gate is the Holy One of Israel; and he employeth no servant there." (2 Nephi 9:41.) The Lord, as Gatekeeper, tried to bring temple ordinances to his early people so that they could dwell with him. In our day, the temple, and the accompanying offer to dwell with the Lord, have been restored. Since the temple is the gate of heaven, we must walk through its doors and receive ordinances before we can dwell with Christ in the way he intends for us. We must make and keep sacred temple covenants.

Temple Ordinances

When the Lord told Moses to prepare a second set of stone tables, he said, "I will write upon them also, the words of the law, according as they were written at the first on the tables which thou brakest; but it shall not be according to the first, for I will take away the priesthood out of their midst; therefore my holy order, and the ordinances thereof, shall not go before them; for my presence shall not go up in their midst, lest I destroy them." (JST, Exodus 34:1.)

Ordinances pertaining to his "holy order" (the Melchizedek priesthood) were thereby taken away from the early Israelites. The tabernacle should have been a true temple where all Israel could have received ordinances and entered into the Lord's presence, for he was there.

The difference between the two sets of tables was clarified by the Lord. "I will write on the tables the words that were in the first tables which thou brakest, save the words of the everlasting covenant of the holy priesthood, and thou shalt put them in the ark." (JST, Deuteronomy 10:2.)

This difference was also verified by the Lord to Joseph Smith in September, 1832, in a revelation on priesthood.

> And this greater priesthood administereth the gospel and holdeth the key of the mysteries of the kingdom, even the key of the knowledge of God.
>
> Therefore, in the ordinances thereof, the power of godliness is manifest.
>
> And without the ordinances thereof, and the authority of the priesthood, the power of godliness is not manifest unto men in the flesh;
>
> For without this no man can see the face of God, even the Father, and live.
>
> Now this Moses plainly taught to the children of Israel in the wilderness, and sought diligently to sanctify his people that they might behold the face of God;
>
> But they hardened their hearts and could not endure his presence; therefore, the Lord in his wrath, for his anger was kindled against them, swore that they should not enter into his rest while in the wilderness, which rest is the fulness of his glory.
>
> Therefore, he took Moses out of their midst, and the Holy Priesthood also;
>
> And the lesser priesthood continued. (D&C 84:19–26.)

In October, 1838, the Lord commanded the Saints
in Nauvoo to "build a house to my name, for the Most
High to dwell therein." The temple was not only a
dwelling place for the Lord, but also a place where
ordinances could be restored. "For there is not a
place found on earth that he may come to and restore
again that which was lost unto you, or which he hath
taken away, even the fulness of the priesthood."
(D&C 124:27–28.)

Further emphasis came in ensuing verses. "And
again, verily I say unto you, how shall your washings
be acceptable unto me, except ye perform them in a
house which you have built to my name? For, for this
cause I commanded Moses that he should build a
tabernacle . . . in the wilderness, and to build a house
in the land of promise, that those ordinances might
be revealed which had been hid from before the
world was. . . . And verily I say unto you, let this
house be built unto my name, that I may reveal mine
ordinances therein unto my people." (D&C
124:37–38, 40.)

Comparison of the temple in Nauvoo to the tabernacle in the wilderness was not incidental. Both were
intended to offer necessary ordinances to the house
of Israel. Both had three divisions: the tabernacle
with an outer court, the Holy Place, and the Holy of
Holies; paralleling the telestial, terrestrial, and
celestial rooms of the temple. Most important, both
were to sanctify the people. The ordinances of the
temple prepare us to dwell in the glorious presence of
the Lord.

Covenant Law of Consecration

Just as ordinances given on the two sets of stone
tables were different, so also was the law different.
When the Lord instructed Moses to prepare the sec-

ond set, he specified, "I will give unto them the law as at the first, but it shall be after the law of a carnal commandment." (JST, Exodus 34:2.)

The ten commandments were the same on both tables. Yet the *law* on the tables was different, as indicated by the words "but it shall be after the law of a carnal commandment." In the New Testament, Paul described Christ as a priest "who is made, not after the law of a carnal commandment." (Hebrews 7:16.) He became a higher being by living a higher law. Modern revelation answers how the first law was like the second but was not a carnal commandment.

In 1831, the Lord introduced a revelation by saying, "I am the same which have taken the Zion of Enoch into mine own bosom. . . . Mine eyes are upon you. I am in your midst and ye cannot see me; But the day soon cometh that ye shall see me, and know that I am." (D&C 38:4, 7–8.) In this section the Lord told the Saints to move to Ohio, "and there I will give unto you my law; and there you shall be endowed with power from on high." (D&C 38:32.) Being "endowed with power from on high" we recognize as ordinances in the Kirtland temple. But these were two separate gifts. The first gift was "my law."

On February 9, 1831, that promised law was given to Joseph Smith in Kirtland, Ohio. "Thou shalt not kill. . . . Thou shalt not steal. . . . Thou shalt not lie. . . . Thou shalt not commit adultery. . . ." (D&C 42:18–27.) These were familiar; this was the law binding on all people at all times. In fact, the Lord said, "Thou knowest my laws concerning these things." (D&C 42:28.)

These were the prerequisites to the more difficult part of the law. Next came: "And behold, thou wilt remember the poor, and consecrate of thy properties for their support that which thou hast to impart unto them, with a covenant and a deed which cannot be broken." (D&C 42:30.) This law was administered by covenant. Today we call this the law of consecration.

The Lord referred to the Zion of Enoch in Section 38 preparatory to restoring the law of consecration because the people there lived this covenant law. "And the Lord called his people Zion, because they were of one heart and one mind, and dwelt in righteousness; and there was no poor among them." (Moses 7:18.) This was one important reason why Zion was taken up to live in heaven. In order for the Saints of the latter day to receive the same blessing as the early Saints, they must live the same law.

In March of 1832, the Lord gave further instruction, "that you may be equal in the bonds of heavenly things, yea, and earthly things also, for the obtaining of heavenly things. . . . For if you will that I give unto you a place in the celestial world, you must prepare yourselves by doing the things which I have commanded you and required of you . . . who are joined together in this order" or covenant law of consecration. (D&C 78:5–8.)

The revelation continued. "Wherefore, a commandment I give unto you, to prepare and organize yourselves by a bond or everlasting covenant that cannot be broken." (D&C 78:11.) The Lord went on to specify "this is the preparation wherewith I prepare you," for "ye have not as yet understood how great blessings the Father hath in his own hands and prepared for you." (D&C 78:13, 17.) In other words, this highest law prepared the Saints for the highest blessings.

Christ gave us a brief glimpse of the great blessings to follow the preparation. "The kingdom is yours and the blessings thereof are yours, and the riches of eternity are yours." (D&C 78:18.) He promised to lead us along, for he is the Redeemer "who prepareth all

things before he taketh you; . . . he will take you up
in a cloud." (D&C 78:20–21.) One of the early
rewards, then, for faithfully living the law of consecration is to be taken up in a cloud at Christ's coming
to dwell with him. The "riches of eternity" follow.

The Choice

The Lord fully renewed his offer for man to dwell
with him, validating that offer for us today. In our
time he carefully restored the ordinances and the
covenant law which are necessary to prepare the
way.

For us to be taken up in a cloud, with other blessings to follow, the Lord was not concerned about temple ordinances alone, as essential as they are. He
was saying that if we want to live *where* he lives, we
must live *as* he lives. Heavenly law requires consecration by covenant. Those who have received their
priesthood endowment see how the two connect.
Through the example of the City of Enoch and
through instruction in our day, the relationship of
living the law of consecration to dwelling with the
Lord is clear.

The offer to the people of Enoch was the same as
the offer to the people of Moses. This offer is restored
to us. By receiving temple ordinances and by obeying
covenant law, we will enjoy the blessings of living
with our Savior in his glory. The offer is valid; the
choice to accept or reject is now ours.

13

SHECHINAH PROPHECY— THE SECOND COMING

After we have received a baptism of fire and have received the ordinances and covenants of the temple, we look forward to the Second Coming of Jesus Christ. We eagerly anticipate him because the covenant relationship is in order. He will be our God, and we are preparing to be his people.

Sign of Second Coming

We are told to watch for the Second Coming of Christ, and we are told that when he comes, "immediately there shall appear a great sign in heaven, and all people shall see it together." (D&C 88:93.) How shall we watch for this sign if we do not know what it is? Or how shall we recognize it when we see it if we have never heard of it? The New Testament also teaches us to watch, that after tribulation, "then shall appear the sign of the Son of man in heaven." (Matthew 24:30.) What is this sign?

The verse goes on, "And then shall all the tribes of the earth mourn, and they shall see the Son of man coming in the clouds of heaven with power and great glory." (Matthew 24:30; see also Joseph Smith— Matthew 1:36.) That is it! The sign of the Son of Man is not first and separate from his coming in the clouds. It is one and the same. The sign of the Son of Man, the sign of his coming, is the Shechinah.

Christ's glorious coming is also described in two other gospels. "And then shall they see the Son of man coming in the clouds with great power and glory." (Mark 13:26.) This description is almost identical with the one in Luke, "And then shall they see the Son of man coming in a cloud with power and great glory." (Luke 21:27.) Matthew adds this detail: "For as the lightning cometh out of the east, and shineth even unto the west; so shall also the coming of the Son of man be." (Matthew 24:27.) By "lightning," Matthew means the lighting up of the sky at sunrise. The Pearl of Great Price clarifies this meaning and inserts a phrase. "For as the light of the morning cometh out of the east, and shineth even unto the west, and covereth the whole earth, so shall also the coming of the Son of Man be." (Joseph Smith—Matthew 1:26.) Thus four accounts bear witness of the sign. In addition, after Christ's ascension into heaven in a cloud, the angel testified that he would return in "like manner." The New Testament tells us clearly what to watch for.

It is important that we know what to watch for because the world will not recognize the sign. Joseph Smith taught, "Then will appear one grand sign of the Son of Man in heaven. But what will the world do? They will say it is a planet, a comet, etc. But the Son of Man will come as the sign of the coming of the Son of Man, which will be as the light of the morning cometh out of the east." (Smith, *Teachings of the Prophet Joseph Smith*, p. 287.) We somehow expect everyone, ourselves included, to automatically recognize this sign without knowing what it is. However, without understanding the manifestation of the Lord's presence, the citizens of Kirtland simply saw a building in flames. We must watch, then, for the Shechinah.

In our day the Lord began early to teach the Saints the manner of his coming. In 1830, when the Church was only five months old, he taught, "I will reveal myself from heaven with power and great glory, with all the hosts thereof, and dwell in righteousness with men on earth a thousand years." (D&C 29:11.) References like this are easy to miss unless we know what "power and great glory" means. We see here, too, the original intent of the sign, that is, the Lord coming to dwell with man.

Six weeks later, the Lord, through Joseph Smith, called Orson Pratt to preach the gospel, "preparing the way of the Lord for his second coming. For . . . the time is soon at hand that I shall come in a cloud with power and great glory." (D&C 34:6–7.) This is a clear reference to the Shechinah. In essence, we all have the same responsibility as Orson Pratt.

To help us prepare, Christ told of his early disciples who asked "concerning the signs of my coming, in the day when I shall come in my glory in the clouds of heaven, to fulfil the promises that I have made unto your fathers." (D&C 45:16.) Christ used this as an introduction to explain future events.

> When they shall see all these things, then shall they know that the hour is nigh. And it shall come to pass that he that feareth me shall be looking forth for the great day of the Lord to come, even for the signs of the coming of the Son of Man. And they shall see signs and wonders, for they shall be shown forth in the heavens above, and in the earth beneath. And they shall behold blood, and fire, and vapors of smoke. . . . And then they shall look for me, and, behold, I will come; and they shall see me in the clouds of heaven, clothed with power and great glory. (D&C 45:38–42, 44.)

He continued with an implied warning. "And at that day, when I shall come in my glory, shall the parable be fulfilled which I spake concerning the ten virgins." (D&C 45:56.) Of the ten virgins, all of whom represent the Church membership, half were unprepared. To watch and wait is not enough; we must be prepared.

Malachi also knew the importance of personal readiness. He prophesied, "The Lord, whom ye seek, shall suddenly come to his temple." (Malachi 3:1.) The critical word is "suddenly." Realizing the danger of not being worthy, he asked, "Who may abide the day of his coming? and who shall stand when he appeareth? for he is like a refiner's fire, and like fullers' soap." (Malachi 3:2; 3 Nephi 24:2.) In other words, his fire is both a purifier and a cleanser.

The Fire of God As a Destructive Power

While the fire of God purifies the righteous, it destroys the wicked. Actually only one process is happening: the purging of filthiness. Once filthiness is burned from the evil, however, nothing remains, leaving them destroyed. The Holy Ghost, in a baptism of fire, burns the dross from the righteous. In a parallel baptism of fire, at the Second Coming the earth will be cleansed from dross by burning the wicked. The Lord's burning of the earth is similar to a farmer burning his fields to prepare for a better future yield. This comparison clarifies why Jesus taught that the wheat will be gathered while the tares will be burned. (See Matthew 13:24–30; D&C 86:1–7.) Christ clearly states, "In that day will I send mine angels to pluck out the wicked and cast them into unquenchable fire." (D&C 63:54.)

The psalmist knew that fire would create great destruction at the Second Coming of the Messiah. "Clouds and darkness are round about him: . . . A fire goeth before him, and burneth up his enemies round about. His lightnings enlightened the world: the earth saw, and trembled. The hills melted like wax

at the presence of the LORD, . . . and all the people
see his glory." (Psalms 97:2–6.)

Through visions, Isaiah knew of destruction
attending the Savior's final coming. "Thou shalt be
visited of the LORD of hosts with thunder, and with
earthquake, and great noise, with storm and tem-
pest, and the flame of devouring fire." (Isaiah 29:6;
2 Nephi 27:2.) Isaiah forewarned, "The LORD will
come with fire, and with his chariots like a whirlwind, to render his anger with fury, and his rebuke
with flames of fire." (Isaiah 66:15.)

Destruction by fire with hail is foretold for the
last days. In Pharaoh's day, "the LORD sent thunder
and hail, and the fire ran along upon the ground. . . .
So there was hail, and fire mingled with the hail,
very grievous." (Exodus 9:23–25.) As a type, the
plague will shortly be duplicated on a greater scale.
Ezekiel prophesied that the Lord will plead for
repentance "with pestilence and with blood; and I
will rain . . . an overflowing rain, and great hail-
stones, fire, and brimstone." (Ezekiel 38:22.) John
the Revelator likewise foresaw "hail and fire mingled with blood." (Revelation 8:7.) This is a sign
pointing to the coming of the Lord because John saw
this destruction after the seventh seal had been
opened but before the Second Coming.

Close to the time of fulfillment, modern day prophesies contain numerous fiery warnings. Not only man
but also "every corruptible thing" including beast,
fowl, and fish, "shall be consumed . . . [and] element
shall melt with fervent heat." (D&C 101:24–25.) "Element" is the earth itself, not being destroyed but purified according to other prophecies.

Destroying the wicked serves another purpose. As
the Lord proclaims, "By the fire of mine indignation
will I preserve [the righteous]." (D&C 35:14.) However,
Christ warns even Zion that "if she observe not to do

whatsoever I have commanded her, I will visit her according to all her works, with sore affliction, . . . with devouring fire." (D&C 97:26.)

Lifted Up at the Last Day

To be lifted up means to meet Christ in the cloud at his coming. Worthiness to be in his presence is required; men are either lifted up or destroyed. Being lifted up is a certainty for those who keep the law of consecration.

This blessing was first mentioned in New Testament times. Paul taught, "Then we which are alive and remain shall be caught up together with them in the clouds, to meet the Lord in the air: and so shall we ever be with the Lord." (1 Thessalonians 4:17.)

The Book of Mormon often reiterated the blessing. Alma advised our obedience, adding, "If ye do these things, ye shall be lifted up at the last day." (Alma 37:37.)

Modern revelation abounds with the promise, often coupled with an admonition. The Lord proclaimed, "Gird up your loins and be faithful, and ye shall overcome all things, and be lifted up at the last day." (D&C 75:22.)

The righteous dead qualify for the same blessing. The Lord said, "the saints that have slept shall come forth to meet me in the cloud." (D&C 45:45.) The same promise was repeated in a later revelation. "They who have slept in their graves shall come forth, for their graves shall be opened; and they also shall be caught up to meet him in the midst of the pillar of heaven." (D&C 88:97.) The words *cloud* and *pillar of heaven* both describe the Shechinah.

Countless references in the Old Testament, New Testament, Book of Mormon, and Doctrine and Covenants confirm that fire, simultaneously destroying and refining, will accompany the long-awaited arrival. The scriptures clearly testify that Jesus Christ will return at his Second Coming in great glory. The Shechinah is the sign of the Son of Man. Watch for it, and be ready.

14

SHECHINAH PROPHECY—
THE CITIES OF ZION

When Christ comes to claim his kingdom, he will have two great capitals: Zion in America, and Zion in Jerusalem. Long ago Isaiah knew this and lamented his time. "Thy holy cities are a wilderness, Zion is a wilderness, Jerusalem a desolation." (Isaiah 64:10.) Zion, in America, was not yet built, and Jerusalem had been destroyed. Both cities will be built and ready prior to the Lord's coming. Both cities will have a temple. Once Christ is King, out of Jerusalem will come the "the word of the Lord," and from Zion will come "the law." (Micah 4:2.) Both cities will be full of his glory, for this is the long-awaited millennial reign.

At least four groups of covenant people have already tried to build Zion. When the Lord gathered his people out of Egypt, his intention was to build a Zion where he could dwell among them. The children of Israel and the City of Enoch received the same opportunity. The people of Enoch succeeded and the children of Israel did not. The Book of Mormon suggests that the Nephites enjoyed a Zion society during the two hundred years following Christ's appearance. In Joseph Smith's time, the Saints attempted to establish Zion in Missouri, but, like the children of Israel, they failed. The Saints in Peter's day apparently also tried and failed. We can learn from these efforts and, as a result, be among those who build the next Zion to dwell with Christ.

Duplication of Events

The Saints in the latter days learned early that Zion would be built in Missouri. In February, 1834, Parley P. Pratt and Lyman Wight came to Joseph Smith in Ohio to discuss lands in Jackson County. Knowing the pattern, the Lord gave them this comforting promise: "As your fathers were led at the first, even so shall the redemption of Zion be. Therefore, let not your hearts faint, for I say not unto you as I said unto your fathers: Mine angel shall go up before you, but not my presence. But I say unto you: Mine angels shall go up before you, and also my presence, and in time ye shall possess the goodly land." (D&C 103:18–20.) This was a clear reference to the Israelites obtaining their promised land in Moses' day. In the same manner that the Lord led them "at the first," he will lead us when we go to claim Zion.

Moses reminded the children of Israel that the Lord "went in the way before you, to search you out a place to pitch your tents in, in fire by night, to shew you by what way ye should go, and in a cloud by day." (Deuteronomy 1:33.) Isaiah saw a parallel in the latter days. After Zion is washed and Jerusalem is purged "by the spirit of burning . . . the LORD will create upon every dwelling place of mount Zion . . . a cloud and smoke by day, and the shining of a flaming fire by night; for upon all the glory shall be a defence." (Isaiah 4:4–5; 2 Nephi 14:5.) This describes Zion, defended as Israel of old.

Orson Pratt prophesied of the Lord going before a latter day march. "When we go back [to build Zion] there will be a very large organization consisting of thousands, and tens of thousands, and they will march forward, the glory of God overshadowing their camp by day in the form of a cloud, and a pillar of flaming fire by night, the Lord's voice being uttered forth before his army. . . . Will not this produce terror upon all the nations of the earth?" (*Journal of Discourses* 15:364.) The Shechinah will be leading at the last, as "at the first."

Enoch and his people

Included in the holy City of Zion will be Enoch and his people. The Lord implied their return when he said they "were separated from the earth, and were received unto myself—a city reserved until a day of righteousness shall come." (D&C 45:12.) A later revelation specified, "The Lord hath redeemed his people. . . . The Lord hath brought down Zion from above [City of Enoch], The Lord hath brought up Zion from beneath [New Jerusalem]." (D&C 84:100.)

The clearest prophecy that the two cities shall unite is the promise to Enoch that Christ would prepare a "Holy City, that my people may . . . be looking forth for the time of my coming . . . and it shall be called Zion, a New Jerusalem. And the Lord said unto Enoch: Then shalt thou and all thy city meet them there, and we will receive them into our bosom, and they shall see us; and we will fall upon their necks, and they shall fall upon our necks, and we will kiss each other." (Moses 7:62–63.)

The two Zions will become one, watching together for the sign of the Son of Man. In fact, the uniting of these two righteous cities signals his imminent coming.

The Millennial Reign

As Enoch foresaw, Christ will reign from Zion. "And there shall be mine abode, and it shall be Zion. . . . [And] Enoch saw the day of the coming of the Son

of Man, in the last days, to dwell on the earth in
righteousness for the space of a thousand years."
(Moses 7:64–65.)

Finally, after some six thousand years, the Creator, Savior, and Mediator will come to earth to dwell
with a people prepared to meet him. What a joyful
day!

Temples in the Cities of Zion

The temples in Zion and Jerusalem will house the
Lord's holy presence, and many great prophecies will
be fulfilled. Isaiah foretold that in the Jerusalem
temple, "Flocks [and] rams. . . shall minister unto
thee: they shall come up with acceptance on mine
altar, and I will glorify the house of my glory." (Isaiah
60:7.) This shows a restoration of animal sacrifice,
which will also be offered in the New Jerusalem temple. (See D&C 84:31.) Most important in the prophesy, however, is the restoration of the glory of the
Lord.

In September, 1832, the Lord revealed that the
"city New Jerusalem shall be built . . . beginning at
this place [western Missouri] even the place of the
temple, which temple shall be reared in this generation. For verily . . . an house shall be built unto the
Lord, and a cloud shall rest upon it, which cloud
shall be even the glory of the Lord, which shall fill
the house." (D&C 84:4–5.) Thus, the Shechinah, indicating the presence of the Lord, will attend both temples.

The Lord gave another promise concerning the
temple in August, 1833. "Verily I say unto you, that
it is my will that a house should be built unto me in
the land of Zion [Jackson County]. . . . [And] my glory
shall rest upon it; Yea, and my presence shall be
there, for I will come into it, and all the pure in heart

that shall come into it shall see God." (D&C 97:10, 15–16.) This was a promise like that given for the temple of Solomon. As that promise came to pass, so will this one. Orson Pratt, speaking of the temple to be built in Missouri, gave a vivid description of this same promise.

> I will tell you another thing that will happen in our promised land, after that temple is built: there will a cloud of glory rest upon that temple by day, the same as the cloud rested upon the tabernacle of Moses, that was carried in the wilderness. Not only that, but also a flaming fire will rest upon the temple by night, covering the whole temple; and if you go inside of the temple, the glory of God will be seen there as it was anciently; for the Lord will not only be a glory and a defense on the outside of that wonderful building, but he will also be a glory and a power in the inside thereof, and it shall come to pass that every man and every woman who is pure in heart, who shall go inside of that temple, will see the Lord. Now, how great a blessing it will be to see the Lord of Hosts as we see one another in the flesh. That will take place, but not till after the temple is built. *(Journal of Discourses* 21:330.)

Christ In the Midst of Zion

Isaiah, envisioning the joy of Christ dwelling with Zion, exulted, "Cry out and shout, thou inhabitant of Zion: for great is the Holy One of Israel in the midst of thee." (Isaiah 12:6.)

In September, 1831, Joseph Smith learned that "the Lord shall be in [Zion's] midst and his glory shall be upon [the people], and he will be their king and their lawgiver." (D&C 45:56–59.) More detail of the glorious city was revealed a year later. "The heavens have smiled upon her; And she is clothed with the glory of her God; For he stands in the midst of his people." (D&C 84:101.)

Seeing Christ in the temple is an incomprehensible blessing, yet having him in our midst is even greater. The prophet Zechariah rejoiced at the prospect. "Sing and rejoice, O daughter of Zion: for, lo, I come, and I will dwell in the midst of thee, saith the LORD. And many nations shall be joined to the LORD in that day, and shall be my people: and I will dwell in the midst of thee." (Zechariah 2:10–11.)

Lorenzo Snow prophesied, "Many of you will be living in Jackson County . . . and you may expect . . . to see Him, to eat and drink with Him, to shake hands with Him and to invite Him to your houses as He was invited when He was here before." (Lundwall, *Temples of the Most High,* p. 209–210.)

President Snow's prophecy adds literal meaning to the following revelation: "For I, the Lord, have put forth my hand to exert the powers of heaven; ye cannot see it now, yet a little while and ye shall see it, and know that I am, and that I will come and reign with my people." (D&C 84:119.) He will not be an uninvolved absentee king but an ever-present personal king, mingling with us.

Light of Zion

Isaiah foresaw the light that will illuminate Zion. He called for Zion to "Arise, shine; for thy light is come, and the glory of the LORD is risen [shining] upon thee. For behold, the darkness shall cover the earth, and gross darkness the people: but the LORD shall arise [shine] upon thee, and his glory shall be seen upon thee. And the Gentiles shall come to thy light, and kings to the brightness of thy rising [shining]." (Isaiah 60:1–3.) The glorious light of Zion will come from the Lord.

John the Revelator knew this, for he wrote, "The city had no need of the sun, neither of the moon, to shine in it: for the glory of God did lighten it, and the Lamb is the light thereof." (Revelation 21:23.) In fact, modern revelation states, "So great shall be the glory of his presence that the sun shall hide his face in shame, and the moon shall withhold its light." (D&C 133:49.) John also wrote, "There shall be no night there; and they need no candle . . . for the Lord God giveth them light." (Revelation 22:5.)

Orson Pratt described the reaction of nations to the far-reaching light of Zion. "The light will shine so conspicuously from that city, extending to the very heavens that . . . it will have quite a tendency to strike terror to all the nations of the earth. . . . Some of these kings and nobles, when they see the light shining forth like the northern lights in the arctic regions, illuminating the whole face of the heavens— when they see this light shining forth long before they reach the city, fear will take hold of them. . . . They will try to haste away from the glory of God and from the power of God, and to get out of the country as soon as possible." (Crowther, *Prophecy— Key to the Future*, p. 115; italics omitted; quoting from *Journal of Discourses* 24:29.)

Prophecies of the cities of Zion emphasize the Shechinah. The cloud by day and the fire by night will protect Zion as at the first. The glory of the Lord will fill the temples and be upon the people. Even the light for the cities will come from the Divine Presence. For the people of the Lord who live there, how splendid Zion will be.

15

DIVINE PROMISES

Christ's deep desire is for us to become like him. With infinite love he has prepared the way. Christ has also *shown* us the way by example. He said, "What manner of men ought ye to be? Verily I say unto you, even as I am." (3 Nephi 27:27.) This requires our obeying the laws and ordinances of the gospel which he gave us. When our offering plus Christ's sacrifice pay the price, the divine promises and purposes can be achieved. He explained, "this is my work and my glory—to bring to pass the immortality and eternal life of man." (Moses 1:39.)

Paul summarized who we are and what Christ offers us. He wrote that we are "Israelites; to whom pertaineth the adoption, and the glory, and the covenants, and the giving of the law, and the service of God, and the promises." (Romans 9:4.) Keeping the covenants and the law, along with giving service, precede receiving the promises and the glory. But the promises are great—*we* can receive glory.

Somehow we must make the transition from believing intellectually that man can receive glory to believing emotionally that it is possible for us personally. Attaining celestial glory is not impossible: neither is it possible only for someone else. But we need both faith in ourselves (an attitude that I *can* do it) and heartfelt determination (committment that says I *will* do it) to win the eternal prize. Our hope and faith come through believing Christ's promise: "If ye are faithful ye shall be . . . crowned with honor, and glory, and immortality, and eternal life." (D&C 75:5.) Progressive evidence of the reality of succeeding can help us visualize our own eventual triumph.

We See God

The scriptures testify that the righteous will actually see God. "Verily, thus saith the Lord: It shall come to pass that every soul who forsaketh his sins and cometh unto me, and calleth on my name, and obeyeth my voice, and keepeth my commandments, shall see my face and know that I am." (D&C 93:1.)

The Lord also said, "Therefore, sanctify yourselves that your minds become single to God, and the days will come that you shall see him; for he will unveil his face unto you, and it shall be in his own time, and in his own way, and according to his own will." (D&C 88:68.) The obedient shall see God, for it is his promise to them.

Vision of Heaven

Living with God is a real and personal possibility. Joseph Smith envisioned our heavenly home. "The heavens were opened upon us, and I beheld the celestial kingdom of God, and the glory thereof, . . . I saw the transcendent beauty of the gate through which the heirs of that kingdom will enter, which was like unto circling flames of fire; Also the blazing throne of God, whereon was seated the Father and the Son." (D&C 137:1–3.)

Earlier Joseph Smith taught, "That same sociality which exists among us here will exist among us there, only it will be coupled with eternal glory, which glory we do not now enjoy." (D&C 130:1–2.)

Angels with Glory

That angels from God radiate with his glory is common Christian knowledge. On Easter morning, "The angel of the Lord descended from heaven. . . . His countenance was like lightning, and his raiment white as snow." (Matthew 28:2–3.)

Joseph Smith recorded "a light appearing in my room, which continued to increase until the room was lighter than at noonday." (Joseph Smith—History 1:30.) Joseph described the angel Moroni who "had on a loose robe of most exquisite whiteness. It was a whiteness beyond anything earthly I had ever seen; nor do I believe that any earthly thing could be made to appear so exceedingly white and brilliant. . . . Not only was his robe exceedingly white, but his whole person was glorious beyond description, and his countenance truly like lightning." (Joseph Smith—History 1:31–32.) Moroni, who had once been mortal like us, had received a whiteness and brightness—a glory.

President Joseph F. Smith saw in vision a vast host of departed Saints. He told how their "countenances shone, and the radiance from the presence of the Lord rested upon them." (D&C 138:24.) Thus, multitudes of angels, who once lived on earth, now glow with glory.

Mortals Shining

On occasion, mortals have shone with a heavenly radiance. Enoch's experience was the earliest record of such an event. When he went to talk with the Lord on the mountain, he "was clothed upon with glory." (Moses 7:3.)

On another occasion Moses shone with the glory of God. Paul plainly wrote,"the children of Israel could not stedfastly behold the face of Moses for the glory of his countenance." (2 Corinthians 3:7.) The

Old Testament explains that when Moses came down from talking with God on mount Sinai, "the skin of his face shone; and [the people] were afraid to come nigh him." (Exodus 34:30; see also Exodus 34:35.) So, Moses put a veil on his face to talk to the people and took it off to talk to the Lord.

Moses wrote in third person of his experience. "And he saw God face to face, and he talked with him, and the glory of God was upon Moses; therefore Moses could endure his presence." (Moses 1:2.)

Then, in first person, Moses added, "But now mine own eyes have beheld God; but not my natural, but my spiritual eyes, for my natural eyes could not have beheld; for I should have withered and died in his presence; but his glory was upon me; and I beheld his face, for I was transfigured before him." (Moses 1:11.)

Others who received a heavenly radiance while still mortals, faced adverse circumstances. In ancient America, Abinadi boldly preached to a degenerate king. Afterwards, the people of king Noah "durst not lay their hands on him, for the Spirit of the Lord was upon him; and his face shone with exceeding luster, even as Moses' did while in the mount of Sinai, while speaking with the Lord." (Mosiah 13:5.)

In a prison, Nephi and Lehi were surrounded by hostile Lamanites. Through divine intervention, they were protected by fire. Their faces shone "exceedingly, even as the faces of angels." (Helaman 5:36.)

In the New Testament, Stephen, like Abinadi, confronted a court of accusers. "And all that sat in the council, looking stedfastly on him, saw his face as it had been the face of an angel." (Acts 6:15.) When Stephen was martyred within the hour, he was full of the Holy Ghost and saw a vision of God. Thus, Stephen's face shone.

These six men from scriptures are not the only ones who have shone as mortals. In our own day, "many accounts exist of Joseph [Smith] glowing as though a light were within him when the Holy Ghost came upon him." (Yorgason and Yorgason, *Spiritual Survival in the Last Days,* p. 196; quoting from *Juvenile Instructor.*)

During the Manti Temple dedication in May, 1888, a bright light surrounded the visiting General Authorities. According to one account, a member of the Tabernacle Choir saw twenty-four brethren "encircled by a brightness which appeared to emanate from their own persons. . . .The light followed every movement made by them." (Heinerman, *Temple Manifestations,* p. 121; quoting from *Millennial Star,* March 20, 1896, pp. 205–206.) After turning to tell a friend, the singer discovered the vision closed.

Joseph Smith taught, "Through the power and manifestation of the Spirit, while in the flesh, they [who have the Holy Ghost] may be able to bear [the Lord's] presence in the world of glory." (D&C 76:118.) We probably have many among us who are shining with the Holy Ghost. But our mortal eyes do not usually see this spiritual quality.

Eternal Glory Won

Our level of obedience determines the level of eternal glory we attain. We can receive glory without receiving the fulness, for the telestial, terrestrial, and celestial are all kingdoms of glory. Those who live in the celestial kingdom "shall dwell in the presence of God and his Christ forever and ever." (D&C 76:62.) These are they "whose bodies are celestial, whose glory is that of the sun, even the glory of God, the highest of all." (D&C 76:70.)

Celestial glory can be won. Our foremost example of one gaining it is our elder brother, Jesus. He once lived on earth as we now do, and we rightly worship him for the God of glory that he has become. The scriptures that reveal his godhood also show him mastering eternity step by step through obedience.

There is scriptural proof that the righteous can attain godly glory. Through a vision in Babylon, Daniel saw Adam "whose garment was white as snow, and the hair of his head like the pure wool: his throne was like the fiery flame, and his wheels as burning fire. A fiery stream issued and came forth from before him." (Daniel 7:9–10.) Adam had obtained a shining glory, coupled with a throne.

Speaking of his apostles, Jesus prayed in Gethsemane, "The glory which thou gavest me I have given them." (John 17:22.) Joseph Smith commented that this scripture "shows most clearly that the Savior wished his disciples to understand that they were to be partakers with him in all things, not even his glory excepted." (Lundwall, *Lectures on Faith*, p. 151.) In our time Jesus added, "Mine apostles . . . shall stand at my right hand at the day of my coming in a pillar of fire, being clothed with robes of righteousness, with crowns upon their heads, in glory even as I am, to judge the whole house of Israel." (D&C 29:12.) They could not have glory, even as his, unless they were worthy and it was given to them.

In a revelation showing how exaltation is gained, the Lord plainly told of three who have already achieved it. The first is Abraham, who "hath entered into his exaltation and sitteth upon his throne." (D&C 132:29.) The others are Isaac and Jacob, who, "because they did none other things than that which they were commanded . . . have entered into their exaltation, according to the promises, and sit upon thrones, and are not angels but are gods." (D&C 132:37.)

Although these men were apostles and prophets, the same rewards are available to each of us. The Lord spoke to all ordinary members of the Church when he said, "[I] delight to honor those who serve me in righteousness and in truth unto the end. Great shall be their reward and eternal shall be their glory." (D&C 76:5–6.)

Speaking of one early Church member, the Lord said, "I have seen the work which he hath done, which I accept if he continue, and will crown him with blessings and great glory." (D&C 124:17.) The important word is "if." That this Church member later fell away shows the risk. Nevertheless, the promise of celestial glory is ours if we are diligent unto the end.

Exaltation Sealed

The revelation showing our ancient fathers with exaltation disclosed one more who was worthy: Joseph Smith. "I am the Lord thy God, . . . verily I seal upon you your exaltation, and prepare a throne for you in the kingdom of my Father, with Abraham your father." (D&C 132:49.) This is an account of having exaltation sealed upon or earned by a person yet living. The reward was achieved not received; the throne was prepared and reserved, not bestowed. The sealing acts as a guarantee. Exaltation is godhood (See D&C 132:37), and a fullness of glory is its symbol.

To have exaltation sealed upon us while living seems even more impossible than to achieve it in the next life. Yet there are those who have received it quietly, privately. In fact, Peter exhorted the early Saints to strive for this blessing, which we refer to as making your calling and election sure. To receive a "more sure word of prophecy" is the same thing. The Lord said, "The more sure word of prophecy means a man's knowing that he is sealed up unto eternal life, by revelation and the spirit of prophecy, through the power of the Holy Priesthood." (D&C 131:5.)

Peter gave a concise but clear sermon on the subject. He said that the divine power of our Savior Jesus

Christ has given to us "all things that pertain unto life and godliness, through the knowledge of him that hath called us to glory and virtue: Whereby are given unto us exceeding great and precious promises: that by these ye might be partakers of the divine nature." (2 Peter 1:3–4.) Peter then listed virtues for us to develop, and urged, "Give diligence to make your calling and election sure." (2 Peter 1:10.) As an example to follow, he indicated that he, James, and John had received this blessing at the transfiguration. (See *Mormon Doctrine*, p. 110 and 2 Peter 1:19.)

The divine promise need not be a distant goal. It is within our reach, "if ye do these things," as Peter taught. (2 Peter 1:10.) According to Bruce R. McConkie, if you get on the straight and narrow path and are "pressing forward, and you die, you'll never get off the path. There is no such thing as falling off the straight and narrow path in the life to come, . . . because this is the time and day appointed, this is the probationary estate . . . and, for all practical purposes, your calling and election is made sure." (Yorgason and Yorgason, *Spiritual Survival in the Last Days*, p. 269–270; quoting from an address at the University of Utah.) Elder McConkie makes divine promises sound attainable, and they are.

We Receive Glory

The possibility of our personally receiving glory was known anciently. Abraham knew that "they who keep their first estate shall be added upon; and they who keep not their first estate shall not have glory in the same kingdom with those who keep their first estate; and they who keep their second estate shall have glory added upon their heads for ever and ever." (Abraham 3:26.)

Paul understood, too, when he wrote, "Whereby he called you by our gospel, to the obtaining of the

glory of our Lord Jesus Christ." (2 Thessalonians
2:14.) In others words, the purpose of the gospel is
for us to obtain the glory which Christ has. Paul also
wrote, "We are the children of God: And if children,
then heirs; heirs of God, and joint-heirs with Christ;
if so be that we suffer with him, that we may be also
glorified together. For I reckon that the sufferings of
this present time are not worthy to be compared with
the glory which shall be revealed in us." (Romans
8:16–18.) Our glorious reward will be far greater
than whatever pain we go through in this life.

The Lord also indicated that we must undergo trials
before we can receive glory. "Ye cannot behold . . . the
design of your God concerning those things which
shall come hereafter, and the glory which shall follow
after much tribulation. For after much tribulation
come the blessings. Wherefore the day cometh that
ye shall be crowned with much glory." (D&C 58:3–4.)
The Lord indicated that the divine promise is fulfilled as we are righteous over time. "You may . . . in
due time receive of his fulness. For if you keep my
commandments you shall receive of his fulness, and
be glorified in me as I am in the Father; therefore, I
say unto you, you shall receive grace for grace."
(D&C 93:19–20.) By countless revelations, the Lord
clearly taught that we can receive heavenly glory.

Even a Fulness

To receive the "celestial glory . . . even a fulness"
(D&C 88:29), one more covenant must be obeyed,
that of eternal marriage. The Lord makes this abso-
lutely clear. "For behold, I reveal unto you a new and
an everlasting covenant; and if ye abide not that
covenant, then are ye damned; . . . And as pertaining
to the new and everlasting covenant, it was instituted for the fulness of my glory; and he that

receiveth a fulness thereof must and shall abide the law." (D&C 132:4–6.)

The law of eternal marriage was "instituted," or established explicitly for us to receive the fulness of his glory. To receive a fulness we must abide the law. Those who do not, "cannot, therefore, inherit my glory." (D&C 132:18; see also D&C 132:21.) They may inherit glory, but not Christ's glory. Those who marry by the new and everlasting covenant shall pass "to their exaltation and glory in all things . . . which glory shall be a fulness and a continuation of the seeds forever and ever. Then shall they be gods, because they have no end." (D&C 132:19–20.)

From ages long ago, the Lord's promise to Abraham echoes, "I will multiply thy seed as the stars of the heaven." (Genesis 22:17.)

The Gate of Heaven

One small scripture capsulizes the process of attaining exaltation. "For therein [in the temple] are the keys of the holy priesthood ordained, that you may receive honor and glory." (D&C 124:34.) This is the straight and narrow way to the promised glory: the temple. Clearly, the temple is the gate to our Heavenly Father's celestial home. Nephi emphasized, "There is none other way save it be by the gate." (2 Nephi 9:41.)

By ending with the temple, we have gone full circle. The Shechinah appeared when Jehovah came to bring his temple, his house where the laws and ordinances could be given. Through them, man could enter into the most sacred place, the celestial realm, where the Lord dwelt. Living these celestial laws, man might receive glory from God, becoming like him.

The Shechinah teaches us of Christ—the God of power and great glory. Countless fiery showings testify of Christ guiding us home. The brilliant cloud witnesses his determination to provide us with the covenants and ordinances of exaltation. For now, we prepare for his imminent return in a pillar of fire to claim us. Ultimately we must kneel at the golden mercy seat, pleading for pardon before the Savior. We can eventually attain for ourselves the glory of the Lord, symbolized by the Shechinah. Through the glorious Shechinah, we glimpse not only the Redeemer's power but also his purpose and his plan for our personal perfection and glory.

16

APPLICATION

Eternity seems so far away and exaltation beyond our reach. Here and now, the fog of daily living fuzzes our vision of who we are and what we ought to be and especially of what we can become. Yet the God of glory has said, "I, the Lord, have promised unto you a crown of glory at my right hand." (D&C 104:7.) We must believe him, who is also God of truth.

In reality, our personal path to perfection is simple: "Be thou humble; and the Lord thy God shall lead thee by the hand." (D&C 112:10.) Where do we suppose he will lead us? The answer is irrefutable—home to glory.

After all the scriptures about dwelling with Christ, it finally occurred to me why that is not the real goal. We dwelt with Heavenly Father and our Elder Brother before we came to earth. If our only goal is to return and dwell with them, what have we accomplished by coming to earth? In fact, it would have been preferable to stay with them, so we would not have lost those who fail to return. Instead, we left home so we could mature through experience and achieve our divine inheritance. We came so that we could return with honor and receive glory. Jesus Christ lights our way back home to glory.

In the scriptures, the Shechinah spotlights Christ's Divine Presence and his divine mission. Studying it has made a great impact on me personally. The Sav-

ior is more obvious in my daily life, and I feel closer
to him. Not only do I realize better what he wants me
to do, but also I have a greater desire to do it. Let me
share two experiences.

The first experience occurred in the temple. One
evening as I entered the celestial room, I remem-
bered that in the original temple this room was the
Holy of Holies with the ark of the covenant—the
throne where the Lord could be sitting. To the Jews,
going to the temple meant going to see the Lord.
Surely the Lord has been here, I realized. Where
could I walk without stepping where he has stood? I
resolved to be more worthy.

The second experience happened early one morning when I caught the sunrise in magnificent glory
igniting the sky. Oh! that I could poetically describe
the brilliance—the fiery reds layered with intense
oranges and glowing, golden yellows. The brightness
and color, instead of fading as in a sunset, blazed
more brilliantly and gloriously by the moment, until
sunshine consumed the night and permeated the day.

Instantly, across my mind flashed the prophecy of
the Son of Man coming "as the light of the morning
cometh out of the east. . . . and covereth the whole
earth." (Joseph Smith—Matthew 1:26.) This experience
in nature gave a glimpse of what the prophesied sign
will be like.

One small soul watched the heavenly show testifying that every day the Lord's presence is in our
world. Here was evidence—no, *proof*—for all the
world to see. Literally, "The Lord Is My Light."

The sunshine, though too powerful for us to gaze
on, is a mere token and promise of the light yet to
come, when the Lord in his glory will be here in person. Take time to watch the sunrise and reflect on
what you have learned. Let the glorious message of
the Shechinah change your life.

BIBLIOGRAPHY

Bennett, Archibald F. *Saviors On Mount Zion*. Course No. 21. Salt Lake City: Deseret Sunday School Union Board, 1960.

Crowther, Duane S. *Prophecy—Key to the Future*. Salt Lake City: Bookcraft, In., 1966.

Edmunds, John K. *Through Temple Doors*. Salt Lake City: Bookcraft, Inc., 1978.

Heinerman, Joseph. *Temple Manifestations*. Manti, Ut: Mountain Valley Publishers, 1974.

Hinckley, Bryant S. *Sermons and Missionary Services of Melvin J. Ballard*. Salt Lake City: Deseret Book Company, 1949.

History of the Church. 7 Vols. 2nd edition, Revised. Salt Lake City: The Church of Jesus Christ of Latter-day Saints, 1948.

Hymns. Salt Lake City: The Church of Jesus Christ of Latter-day Saints, 1985.

Jenson, Andrew. *The Historical Record*. Church Encyclopedia, Book 1, Vol. 5, May, 1886. Salt Lake City: 1889.

Journal of Discourses. 26 Vols. Second lithographic reprint. Los Angeles: General Printing and Lithograph Company, 1961.

Lundwall, N. B., comp. *Discourses on the Holy Ghost also Lectures On Faith*. 11th printing. Salt Lake City: Bookcraft, 1975.

Lundwall, N. B. *Temples of the Most High.* Salt Lake City: Bookcraft, Inc., 1947.

McConkie, Bruce R. *Mormon Doctrine.* 2nd paperback printing. Salt Lake City: Bookcraft, Inc., 1981.

Melvin J. Ballard—Crusader for Righteousness. 3rd printing. Salt Lake City: Bookcraft,Inc., 1977.

Olsen, Nolan P. *Logan Temple: The First 100 Years.* 2nd printing. Providence, UT: Keith W. Watkins and Sons, 1979.

Reay, David M., and Vonda S., comps. and pubs. *Selected Manifestations.* Oakland, CA, 1985.

Sandmel, Samuel, ed. *The New English Bible.* New York: Oxford University Press, 1976.

Siegell, Richard, and Strassfeld, Michael, and Sharon, comps. and eds. *The First Jewish Catalog.* Philadelphia: The Jewish Publication Society of America, 1973.

Skousen, W. Cleon. *Fantastic Victory.* Salt Lake City: Bookcraft, Inc., 1967.

Smith, Joseph Fielding. *Doctrines of Salvation.* 3 Vols. Paperback ed. Salt Lake City: Bookcraft, 1954.

Smith, Joseph Fielding, comp. *Teachings of the Prophet Joseph Smith.* Salt Lake City: Deseret Book Company, 1977.

Smith, William. *Smith's Bible Dictionary.* 16th printing. Old Tappan, NJ: Fleming H. Revell Company, 1981.

Sperry, Sidney B. "Ancient Temples and Their Functions." *Improvement Era.* Nov. 1955.

Strassfeld, Sharon, and Michael, comps. and eds. *TheThird Jewish Catalog.* Philadelphia: The Jewish Publication Society of America, 1980.

Talmage, James E. *The House of the Lord*. 4th printing of revised edition. Salt Lake City: Deseret Book Company, 1971.

The New Catholic Study Bible: Today's English Version. Nashville: Thomas Nelson Publishers, 1985.

"The Salt Lake Temple." *Contributor*, Apr.1893, pp. 243-304.

Webster's Ninth New Collegiate Dictionary. Springfield, Ma: Merriam-Webster, 1984.

Yorgason, Blaine and Brenton. *Spiritual Survival in the Last Days*. Salt LakeCity: Ut, 1990.

Zeidner, Ron. *The Jews and the Second Coming*. Audio Tape. Salt Lake City: Covenant Communications, Inc., 1979.

SCRIPTURE INDEX

Explanatory Notes

Scriptures without a letter designation are quoted partially or in full.

Scriptures not quoted are indicated by code:
r—reference. The scripture is referred to.
u—unused. The scripture is unused but refers to the Shechinah.

44: 2, c. 7
44: 4, c. 7
48: 35, c. 7
Daniel
  3: 24–25, c. 7
  7: 9–10, c. 15
  7: 13, c. 7
  9:17 u, c. 7
  10: 5–6, c. 7
Micah
  4: 2, c. 14
  Habakkuk
  3: 3–4 u, c. 7
Haggai
  2: 3–5, c. 7
  2: 7, 9, c. 7
  Zechariah
  2: 10–11 , c. 14
Malachi
  3: 1, c. 7, 13
  3: 2, c. 13

NEW TESTAMENT
Matthew
  3: 11–12, c. 11
  13: 24–30 r, c. 13
  17: 2, c. 8
  17: 5, c. 8
  24: 27, c. 13
  24: 30, c. 13
  26: 63–64, c. 8
  28: 2 3, c. 15
Mark
  9: 2, 7 r, c. 8
  13: 26, c. 13
  14: 61–62 r, c. 8
Luke
  2: 9, c. 8
  2: 32, c. 8
  2: 49, c. 8

3: 16 r, c. 11
7: 16, c. 8
9: 29–32, c. 8
9: 34–35, c. 8
21: 27, c. 13
24: 26, c. 8
John
  1: 14, c. 8
  17: 5, c. 8
  17: 22, c. 15
Acts
  1: 9–11, c. 8
  2: 4, c. 11
  6: 15, c 15
  7: 30, c. 8
  7: 55, c. 8
  9: 3 r, c. 8
  9: 5 r, c. 8
  22: 6, c. 8
  22: 8, c. 8
  22: 11, c. 8
  22: 14–15, c. 8
  26: 13, c. 8
  26: 15 r,
  c. 8
Romans
  8: 16–18, c. 15
  9: 4, c. 15
1 Corinthians
  10: 1, c. 8
2 Corinthians
  3: 7, c. 15
1 Thessalonians
  4: 17, c. 13
2 Thessalonians
  1:7–9 u, c. 13
  2: 8 u, c. 13
  2: 14, c. 15
Hebrews
  1: 2–4, c. 8
  7: 16, c. 12

2 Peter
  1: 3–4, c. 15
  1: 10, c 15
  1: 16–18, c. 8
  1: 19 r, c. 15
Revelation
  1: 7-r, c. 13
  1:12–16, c. 8
  1:18, c. 8
  2: 18 r, c. 8
  8: 7, c. 13
  14: 14 u, c. 13
  15: 8 u, c. 13
  21: 23, c. 14
  22: 5, c. 14

**BOOK OF
MORMON**
1 Nephi
  1: 6, c. 1, 9
  1: 9, c. 9
  17: 30, c. 9
  17: 47, 48, 52, c. 11
2 Nephi
  1:15, c. 9
  2: 4, c. 9
  6: 14 u, c. 13
  9: 41, c. 1, 12, 15
  11: 3, c. 9
  14: 5, c. 14
  27: 2, c. 13
Mosiah
  13: 5, c. 15
Alma
  5: 50 u, c. 9
  9: 26, c. 9
  12:15 u, c. 9
  12: 29 u, c. 9
  13: 24, c. 9
  19: 6, c. 11

SUBJECT INDEX